God's Big Picture

An Overview of God's Developing Story

LET'S KNOW THE BIBLE

God's Big Picture

An Overview of God's Developing Story

Herbert W. Bateman IV

GENERAL EDITOR

Herbert W. Bateman IV * Aaron C. Peer * Timothy D. Sprankle

CC
BS Cyber-Center for Biblical Studies Publication

God's Big Picture: An Overview of God's Developing Story
© 2015 by Herbert W. Bateman IV

Published by Cyber-Center for Biblical Studies, 4078 E. Oldfield Drive, Leesburg, IN.

Let's Know the Bible Conference Material © 2014 by Cyber-Center for Biblical Studies.

Scripture quotations designated NET Bible are from NET BIBLE copyright © 1996-2006 by Biblical Studies Press, L.L.C. http://bible.org. Quoted with permission.

ISBN-13: 978-0-9907797-1-1

Contents

God's Big Picture: An Overview of God's Developing Story in the Bible
Herbert W. Bateman IV

God's Past Story
Timothy D. Sprankle

The Book of Genesis

The Books of Samuel

God's Current Story
Herbert W. Bateman IV

The Book of Matthew

The Book of Romans

God's Future Story
Aaron C. Peer

The Book of Revelation

PREFACE

After accepting Jesus as my savior and king, a desire surfaced within me to learn more about God. What better source is there to turn to than the Bible? A rather significant group of verses that prompted this desire was Philippians 1:9–11 — "And I pray this, that your love may abound even more and more in knowledge and every kind of insight (with this result) so that you can decide what is best, and thus be sincere and blameless for the day of Christ, filled with the fruit of righteousness that comes through Jesus Christ to the glory and praise of God" (NET). What better place to go and learn about the Bible than a Bible college. My eventual enrollment in Philadelphia College of the Bible's degree program (renamed Cairn University) launched a life long study of God's word. But do believers have to go to a Bible college, Christian college, or seminary to learn about God and the Bible?

After serving in the academy for over twenty years, circumstances have afforded me the opportunity to focus more attention to writing and serving local church leaders. Monthly meetings with pastors in Northern Indiana as well as Winona Lake's historical reputation for yearly Bible conferences prompted the idea for a conference that focused attention on the Bible.

Let's Know the Bible conferences exist to provide Bible teaching by leading Christian thinkers and local pastors for church leaders, churchgoers, and others so that people might learn more about God and the Bible and how to navigate everyday life more intentionally. *Let's Know the Bible* is one of several resources created by the Cyber-Center for Biblical Studies to serve pastors and church leaders in their ministries for God.

The Cyber-Center for Biblical Studies is an Internet resource center for pastors, teachers, and seminary students that provides video postings, journal articles, book publications, and "Let's Know the Bible" conferences to serve pastors, church leaders, and students in their ministries for God.

CyberCenterforBiblicalStudies.com

Gratitude must be express to three groups. First, I am grateful for Philadelphia College of the Bible (today Cairn University), the Institute for Holy Land Studies (today Jerusalem University College), Dallas Theological Seminary, and Notre Dame for training, guiding, and honing skills in how to study Scripture as well as insights shared about the Bible gleaned from studying Scripture. These institutions remain committed to offering courses in the Bible that prepare men and women for a life-time of ministry that involves the relevant communication and application of the text for today's world.

Second, gratitude must also be extended to Scott Barger, Aaron Peer, Tim Sprankle, and Jeremy Wike for months of dialogue, suggestions, constructive criticisms, and support for both the launching of the Cyber-Center for Biblical Studies as well as this Let's Know the Bible conference. Their spirit of cooperation and mutual support are models for helping people know God and live as redeemed kingdom saints.

Finally, gratitude must be extended to our sponsors like Kregel Publishing who provided significant financial backing and church sponsors like the people of Leesburg Grace Brethren Church who hosted this year's conference. Thank you.

HERBERT W. BATEMAN IV

CONFERENCE SPEAKERS

HERBERT W. BATEMAN IV

Dr. Herb Bateman, founder of the Cyber-Center for Biblical Studies, has earned his BS in Biblical Studies from Cairn University (1982); his Th.M. (1987) and Ph.D. (1993) in New Testament Studies from Dallas Theological Seminary, and completed postdoctoral study at the University of Notre Dame.

He has been teaching Bible courses in academic institutions since 1986 and within the local church and on the mission field since 1978.

He has taught MDiv and ThM master level students, DMin and PhD level students at Liberty University Theological Seminary, Southwestern Theological Seminary, Grace Theological Seminary, and Dallas Theological Seminary. He has also taught at Asian Theological Seminary in Manila, Philippines and Tyndale Theological Seminary in Amsterdam, Netherlands.

He has spoken at various conferences and written for the church and the academy. Some of his publications include: *Authentic Worship* (Kregel, 2001), *Four Views on the Warning Passages in Hebrews* (Kregel, 2006), *Interpreting the Psalms for Preaching and Teaching* (Chalice, 2010), *Jesus the Messiah* (Kregel, 2012), *Interpreting the General Letters* (Kregel, 2013), and a commentary for the Evangelical Exegetical Commentary series on *Jude* (Logos, 2015).

TIMOTHY D. SPRANKLE

Tim, Senior Pastor at Leesburg Grace Brethren Church in Northern Indiana has earned his BA from Grace College (2001) and MDiv degree from Grace Theological Seminary (2004).

He has taught Bible in academic and church settings since 1995 and pastored for seven years.

He has written, organized, and directed a play for as well as read papers at Meetings of the Regional Midwest Evangelical Theological Society, which have been published in *Authentic Worship* (Kregel 2001), and *Cyber-Center for Biblical Studies eJournal* (2014).

AARON C. PEER

Aaron, Senior Pastor at Charter Oak Church in Churubusco in Northern Indiana has earned his BA from Grace College (2000) and MDiv degree from Grace Theological Seminary (2003).

He has taught Bible in academic and church settings since 1995 and pastored for ten years.

He has taught New Testament Greek and English Bible courses at Grace College and Theological Seminary, assisted in the publication of *A Workbook for Intermediate Greek* (Kregel, 2008) and co-authored *Translating 2 and 3 John Clause by Clause* (Cyber-Center for Biblical Studies, 2014).

God's Big Picture: An Overview of God's Developing Story

Corresponding YouTubes

God's Big Picture: An Overview of God's Developing Story

by *Herbert W. Bateman IV*

YouTube: http://youtu.be/hKHSShoMnhs

QR Code (it stands for "Quick Response") is a mobile phone readable barcode

God's Past Story: Genesis and the Books of Samuel

by *Timothy D. Sprankle*

YouTube: http://youtu.be/MweLyo86tnE

QR Code (it stands for "Quick Response") is a mobile phone readable barcode

Corresponding YouTubes

God's Current Story: Matthew and Romans

by *Herbert W. Bateman IV*

YouTube: http://youtu.be/-by3EMqpsjQ

QR Code (it stands for "Quick Response") is a mobile phone readable barcode

God's Future Story: Revelation

by *Aaron C. Peer*

YouTube: http://youtu.be/S194Cgdk8fM

QR Code (it stands for "Quick Response") is a mobile phone readable barcode

How to Activate the QR Code: Point a mobile phone (or other camera-enabled mobile) at the code. If the device has had QR Code decoding software installed on it, it will fire up its browser and go straight to that URL.

GOD'S BIG PICTURE

An Overview of God's Developing Story in the Bible

by Herbert W. Bateman IV

INTRODUCTION

A. The Bible is a _____ of books.

The Bible is a collection of books that represents different types of _____,

different time periods, different cultures written by numerous _____ authors all of

whom were guided by a _____ author.

B. The Bible paints a picture or tells a _____.

The Bible tells the story about our _____ God and his _____

with the people he created.

Psalm 47 (NET Bible)

All the nations, clap your hands!
    Shout out to God in celebration!
For the sovereign Lord is awe-inspiring,
    He is the great king who rules the whole earth!
He subdued nations beneath us and countries under our feet.
    He picked out for us a special land to be a source of
    pride for Jacob, whom he loves. (Selah)

God has ascended his throne amid loud shouts;
    the Lord has ascended his throne amid the blaring of
    ram's horns.
Sing to God! Sing!

Psalm 24 (NET Bible)

The LORD owns the earth and all it contains,
    the world and all who live in it.
For he set its foundation upon the seas,
    and established it upon the ocean currents.
Who is allowed to ascend the mountain of the LORD?
    Who may go up to his holy dwelling place?
The one whose deeds are blameless
    and whose motives are pure,
    who does not lie,
    or make promises with no intention of keeping them.
Such godly people are rewarded by the LORD,
    and vindicated by the God who delivers them.

Sing to our king! Sing!
For God is king of the whole earth!
Sing a well-written song!
God reigns over the nations!
God sits on his holy throne!
The nobles of the nations assemble,
along with the people of the God of Abraham,
for God has authority over the rulers of the earth.
He is highly exalted!

Such purity characterizes the people who seek his favor,
Jacob's descendants, who pray to him. (Selah)

Look up, you gates!
Rise up, you eternal doors!
Then the majestic king will enter!
Who is this majestic king?
The LORD who is strong and mighty!
The LORD who is mighty in battle!
Look up, you gates!
Rise up, you eternal doors!
Then the majestic king will enter!
Who is this majestic king?
The LORD who commands armies!
He is the majestic king! (Selah)

For Further Reading: Other Psalms also capture God's sovereignty and heavenly enthronement, see Psalms 68, 93, 96, 97, 98, and 99.

C. The Bible, like all books has a _____ and an _____.

Genesis 1:1–2; 2:1–2 (NET Bible)

In the beginning God created the heavens and the earth. Now the earth was without shape and empty, and darkness was over the surface of the watery deep, but the Spirit of God was moving over the surface of the water.

The heavens and the earth were completed with everything that was in them. By the seventh day God finished the work that he had been doing, and he ceased on the seventh day all the work that he had been doing. God blessed the seventh day and made it holy because on it he ceased all the work that he had been doing in creation.

Revelation 21:1–3 (NET Bible)

Then I saw a new heaven and a new earth, for the first heaven and earth had ceased to exist, and the sea existed no more. And I saw the holy city—the new Jerusalem—descending out of heaven from God, made ready like a bride adorned for her husband. And I heard a loud voice from the throne saying: "Look! The residence of God is among human beings. He will live among them, and they will be his people, and God himself will be with them.

God's Strategic Plan Unfolds Linearly through Human History

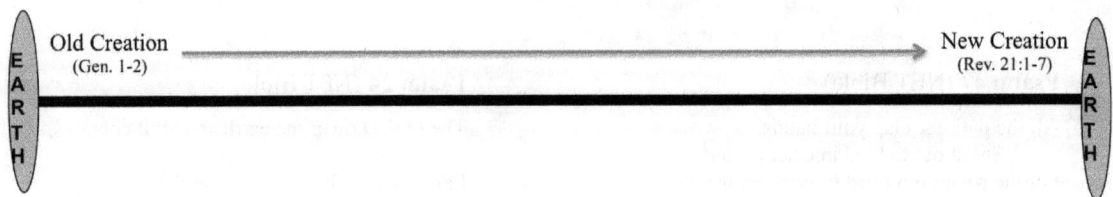

Old Creation (Gen. 1-2) → New Creation (Rev. 21:1-7)

EARTH — EARTH

For Further Reading: For reading about God as creator of the old created order, see Psalms 104, 148; Isaiah 66:22-23. For reading about the new creation of earth, see Revelation 21:1–7; 22:1–4; Romans 8:18–24; 2 Peter 3:13). For reading about followers of Jesus as a new creation, see 2 Corinthians 5:17 and Galatians 6:15.

D. The biblical story is revealed in _____ stages.

1. _____

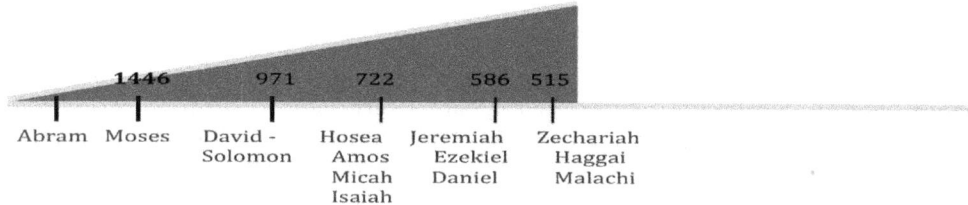

2. _____

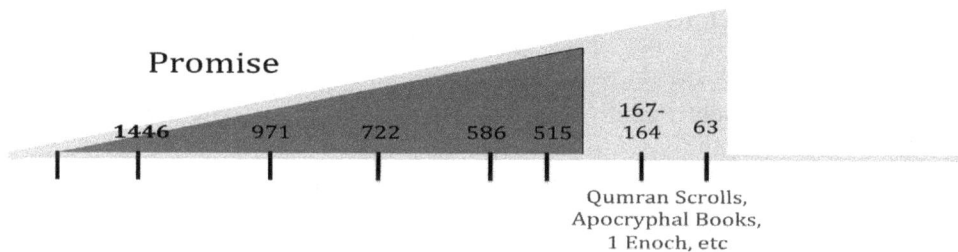

3. Already _____

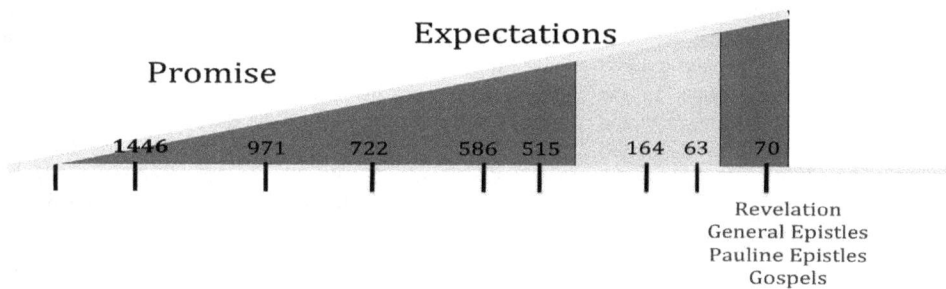

4. Not yet _____

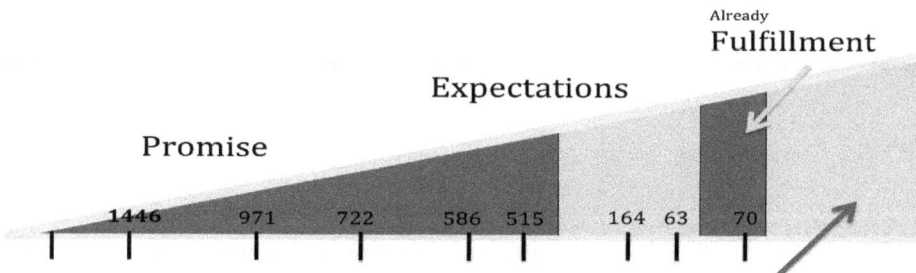

Introduction Summarized: The Bible is a collection of books that has an intentioned beginning and end; that has been written by human authors who have been guided by a divine author; and that tells us, in progressive stages, about our divine king and his relationship with people.

For Further Reading: Each book of the Bible contributes to revealing God's strategically planned desires in a progressive manner through the various stages of human history. The lack of details about God's promises left Abraham scratching his head from time to time (Genesis 15:2–3; 16:1–4, 15–19). Even the prophets did not have all the puzzle pieces (Daniel 12:8–9; Ephesians 3:9). God wanted his people to trust him, though the details of God's program were sketchy.

I.   GOD'S STORY BEGINS WITH A _____

Humanity's Disobedience: People _____ their divine king, and God

issued _____ on them as well as all creation.

Genesis 1:26–28 (NET Bible)

Then God said, "Let us make humankind in our image, after our likeness, *so they may rule* over the fish of the sea and the birds of the air, over the cattle, and over all the earth, and over all the creatures that move on the earth." God created humankind in his own image, in the image of God he created them, male and female he created them. God blessed them and said to them, "Be fruitful and multiply! Fill the earth and subdue it! *Rule* over the fish of the sea and the birds of the air and every creature that moves on the ground.

Genesis 3:6–11 (NET Bible)

When the woman saw that the tree produced fruit that was good for food, was attractive to the eye, and was desirable for making one wise, she took some of its fruit and ate it. She also gave some of it to her husband who was with her, and he ate it. Then the eyes of both of them opened, and they knew they were naked; so they sewed fig leaves together and made coverings for themselves. Then the man and his wife heard the sound of the Lord God moving about in the orchard at the breezy time of the day, and they hid from the Lord God among the trees of the orchard. But the Lord God called to the man and said to him, "Where are you?" The man replied, "I heard you moving about in the orchard, and I was afraid because I was naked, so I hid." And the Lord God said, "Who told you that you were naked? Did you eat from the tree that I commanded you not to eat from?"

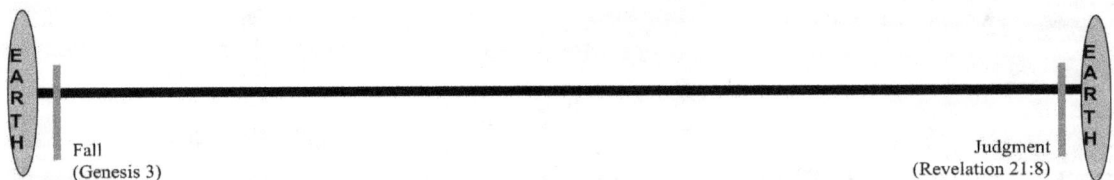

Fall
(Genesis 3)

Judgment
(Revelation 21:8)

Point 1 Summarized: God's story begins with a disruption whereby people disobeyed God, which in turn triggered God's judgment of all creation.

II. GOD'S STORY DEVELOPS A _____

God's (our divine King's) solution is to _____ his kingdom rule on earth

and to _____ a people to enter into that kingdom.

A. Our divine sovereign chooses a _____.

Genesis 12:1–2 (NET Bible)	**Genesis 15:1–2, 4–5** (NET Bible)
Now the Lord said to Abram, "Go out from your country, your relatives, and your father's household to the land that I will show you. Then I will make you into a great nation, and I will bless you, and I will make your name great, in order that you might be a prime example of divine blessing.	After these things the word of the LORD came to Abram in a vision: "Fear not, Abram! I am your shield and the one who will reward you in great abundance." But Abram said, "O Sovereign LORD, what will you give me since I continue to be childless, and my heir is Eliezer of Damascus?" But look, the word of the LORD came to him: "This man will not be your heir, but instead a son who comes from your own body will be your heir." He took him outside and said, "Gaze into the sky and count the stars—if you are able to count them!" Then he said to him, "So will your descendants be."

1. God promised (bilaterally / unconditionally) Abraham a _____, a

   _____ in which Abraham's descendants will dwell, *numerous* _____

   that grows into a _____ *with a royal line*, descendants who will follow

   God, material and spiritual blessings, *mediated* _____ *to other*

   nations through his descendants, namely the nation of Israel, pronounced curses on

   those who persecute Abraham's descendants.

2. God confirmed his promise to Abraham through the birth of _____.

   "The Lord visited Sarah just as he said he would and did for Sarah what he had promised. So Sarah became pregnant and bore Abraham a son in his old age, at the appointed time that God had told him. Abraham named his son — Isaac." Genesis 21:1–3 (NET)

For Further Reading about God's Promised Covenant with Abraham: See God's covenantal promises with Abraham, Sarah and their descendants Isaac, Jacob, and his twelve sons (Isaac: Genesis 26:1–5, 24; Jacob: 27:26–29, 33; 28:13–14; 35:11–12; sons: 49:1–28; cf. Deuteronomy 6:10–15; Jeremiah 31:35–37). Relationship with God during this time, however, involved trusting God, namely, believing what God promised (though the content of promise differed from one person to another), and thereby living and acting in light of the details of promise he understood.

B. Our divine sovereign chooses a _____.

2 Samuel 7:12–16 (NET Bible)

When the time comes for you to die, I will raise up your descendant, one of your own sons, to succeed you, and I will establish his kingdom. He will build a house for my name, and I will make his dynasty permanent. *I will become his father and he will become my son*. When he sins, I will correct him with the rod of men and with wounds inflicted by human beings. But my loyal live will not be removed from him … Your house and your kingdom will stand before me permanently; your dynasty will be permanent.

Psalm 2:1–12 (NET Bible)

Why do the nations cause a commotion?
    Why are the countries devising plots that will fail?
    The kings of the earth form a united front'
    The rulers collaborate against the Lord and his chosen king.
    They say, "Let's tear off the shackles they've put on us!
    Let's free ourselves from their ropes!"

The one enthroned in heaven laughs in disgust,
    The sovereign Master taunts them.
    Then he angrily speaks to them and terrifies them in his rage.
    He says, "I myself have installed my king on Zion, my holy hill."

The king says, "I tell you what the LORD decreed.
    He said to me: "*You are my son!*
    This very day I have become your father!
    You have only to ask me, and I will give you the nations as your inheritance, the ends of the earth your personal property.
    You will break them with an iron scepter;
    you will smash them as if they were a potter's jar."

So now, you kings, do what is wise!"
    You rulers of the earth, submit to correction!
    Serve the LORD in fear!
    Repent in terror!
    Give sincere homage!"

1. God promised (bilaterally / unconditionally) David a Davidic "_____"

   (i.e., posterity, family), an established a "_____" (i.e., royal authority), an

   established "_____" (i.e., a sphere of rule), a _____

   descendant ruling the kingdom.

2. God confirmed his promise to David with _____ enthronement.

   Then Zadok the priest . . . put Solomon on King David's mule, and led him to Gihon. Zadok the priest took a horn filled with oil from the tent and poured it on Solomon; the trumpet was blown and all the people declared, "Long live King Solomon!" Then the king (David) leaned on the bed and said this, "The Lord God of Israel is worthy of praise because today he has placed a successor on my throne and allowed me to see it." 1 Kings 1:38–39, 47b–48 (NET)

For Further Reading: David sees Solomon assume the role as King over Israel (1 Kings 1:28–48; 1 Chronicles 29:10–30; Psalms 2, 110, 132); God promises to restore a Davidic king over a united Israel after Northern Israel was punished for disobedience in 722 B.C. (Isaiah 11:1–5, 10; Amos 9:11–15); God's promise to restore a Davidic king after Judah's exile to Babylon for disobedience in 586 B.C. (Jeremiah 33:14–26; Zechariah 6:12–15; Psalm 89:18–37). Though disobedient, God's covenant made with David endures. People trusted God for a coming Davidic Messiah though the details are sketchy.

C. Our divine sovereign _____ the _____.

Jeremiah 31:31–34 (NET Bible)

"Indeed, a time is coming," says the LORD, "when I will make a new agreement with the people of Israel and Judah. It will not be like the old agreement that I made with their ancestors when I took them out of Egypt. For they violate that agreement, even though I was a faithful husband to them," says the LORD. "But I will make a new agreement with the whole nation of Israel after I plant them back in the land," says the Lord. "I will put my law within them and write it on their hearts and minds. And I will be their God and they will be my people.

People will no longer need to teach their neighbors and relatives (cf. Deuteronomy 6:6–9) to know me. That is because all of them will know me," says the LORD. "All of this is based on the fact that I will forgive their sin and will no longer call to mind the wrong they have done."

Ezekiel 36:24–28 (NET Bible)

"I will take you from the nations and gather yo from all the countries and bring you to you land. I will sprinkle pure water over you and you will be clean from all your uncleanness; I will purify you from all your idols. I will give you a new heart, and I will put a new spirit within you; I will remove the heart of stone from your body and give you a heart of flesh. I will put my spirit within you, and I will make you walk in my statues and keep my ordinances, and you will do them. Then you will live in the land I gave to you fathers; and you will be my people, and I will be your God.

1. God promised (bilaterally / unconditionally) the people of Judah that God's

    expectations will be _____ within the hearts of his people,

    disobedience will be _____, and national resurrection or

    _____ of a united kingdom (Israel and Judah) will occur.

2. God confirmed his promise with his people with the Jewish people's
    _____ from exile.

Ezra 1:1, 5; 2:1 (NET Bible)

In the first year of King Cyrus of Persia . . . the leaders of Judah and Benjamin, along with the priests and the Levites— all those whose mind God had stirred— got ready to go up in order to build the temple of the LORD in Jerusalem." "These are the people of the province who were going up, from the captives of the exile whom King Nebuchadnezzar of Babylon had forced into exile in Babylon."

Haggai 1:1–4, 8, 12–13 (NET Bible)

. . . the LORD spoke this message through the prophet Haggai . . .: The LORD who rules over all says this: "These people have said, 'The time for rebuilding the LORD's temple has not yet come.'" So the LORD spoke through the prophet Haggai as follows: "Is it right for you to live in richly paneled houses while my temple is in ruins?

Go up to the hill country and bring back timber to build the temple. Then I will be pleased and honored,' says the LORD.

. . . the whole remnant of the people, obeyed the LORD their God. They responded favorably to the message of the prophet Haggai, who spoke just as the LORD their God had instructed him, and the people began to respect the LORD. Then Haggai, the LORD's messenger, spoke the LORD's word to the people: "I am with you!" says the LORD.

For Further Reading: People continually looked for the restoration of national Israel (Zechariah 6:11–13; Haggai 2:6). The belief that Israel's national restoration was yet to come even during the time of Jesus is evident in Apocrypha literature (Tobit 14:5–7; Baruch 3:6–8; 2 Maccabees 1:27–29), Qumran literature (CD 1.3–11), and the New Testament (Matthew 24–26; Acts 1:6). The emphasis remains on God's people trusting God, though the details of promise remain sketchy.

Point 2 Summarized: God's resolve to re-establish his kingdom rule on earth and to redeem a people to enter into that kingdom results in a threefold solution whereby God chooses a group of people to mediate his desire, chooses a king from that group of people, and promises to one day change their hearts.

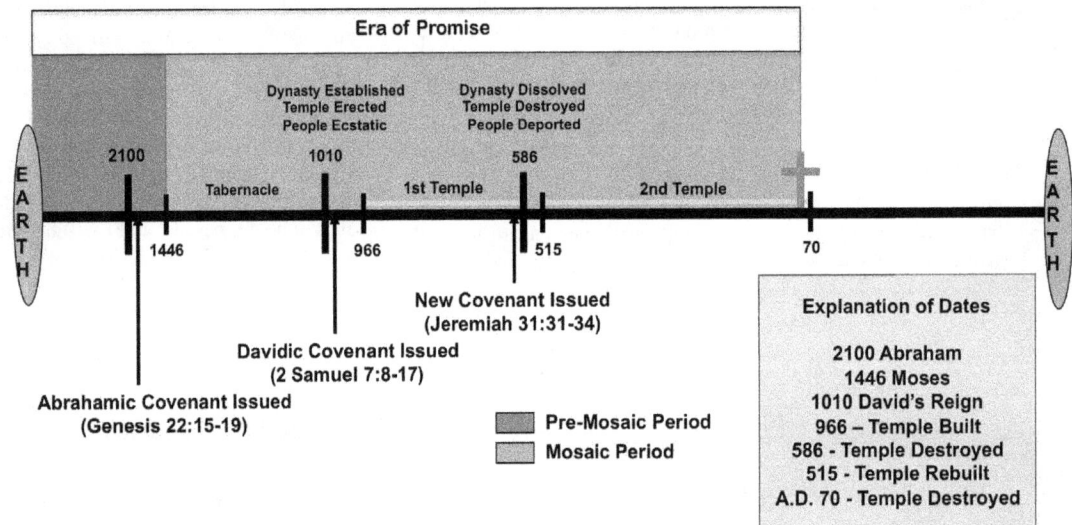

III. GOD'S STORY PROVIDES A _____

A. _____ _____ God's promise to Father Abraham.

Galatians 3:6–9, 16 (NET Bible)

Just as Abraham *believed God, and it was credited to him as righteousness*, so then, understand that those who believe are the sons of Abraham. And the scripture, foreseeing that God would justify the Gentiles by faith, proclaimed the gospel to Abraham ahead of time, saying, "*All the nations will be blessed in you*." So then those who believe are blessed along with Abraham the believer.

Now the promises were spoke to Abraham and to his descendant. Scripture does not say, "and to the descendants," referring to many, but "*and to your descendent*," referring to one, who is Christ.

Romans 4:18 (NET Bible)

Against hope Abraham believed in hope with the result that he became *the father of many nations* according to the pronouncement, "*so will your descendants be*." Without being weak in faith, he considered his own body as dead (because he was about one hundred years old) and the deadness of Sarah's womb. He did not waver in unbelief about the promise of God but was strengthened in faith, giving glory to God. He was fully convinced that what God promised he was also able to do. So indeed it was credited to Abraham as righteousness.

But the statement it was credited to him was not written only for Abraham's sake, but also for our sake, to whom it will be credited, those who believe in the one who raise Jesus our Lord from the dead.

As a descendant of Abraham, Jesus mediates God's blessings to all people and people groups (= nations), namely those who believe that Jesus is the one through God has fulfilled his promises.

For Further Reading: Although Isaac was viewed as the initial child of promise who confirmed God's promise to Abraham (Genesis 21:2–3: Hebrews 11:18–21), the ultimate child of promise through whom God would mediate all of God's covenantal blessings to all people as promised to Abraham is Jesus (compare Hebrews 11:2, 14–17 with Galatians 3:16). God's concern for Abraham's descendents continues (Romans 9–11; Hebrews 2:16; 11:20–22).

B. _____ _____ God's promise to King David.

An angel announced that Jesus was the Davidic king of promise	**Luke 1:30–33** (Net Bible) So the angel said to her, "Do not be afraid, Mary, for you have found favor with God! Listen: You will become pregnant and give birth to a son, and you will name him Jesus. He will be great, and will be called the Son of the Most High, and the Lord God will give him the throne of his father David. He will reign over the house of Jacob forever, and his kingdom will never end."
God proclaimed Jesus to be the Davidic king of promise	**Luke 3:21** (Net Bible) Jesus Baptism: "Now when all the people were baptized, Jesus also was baptized. And while he was praying, the heavens opened, and the Holy Spirit descended on him in bodily form like a dove. And a voice came from heaven, '*You are my one dear Son*; in you I take great delight.'"
	Luke 9:28-35 (Net Bible) Jesus Transfiguration: Jesus took with him Peter, John, and James, and went up the mountain to pray. As he was praying, the appearance of his face was transformed, and his clothes became very bright, a brilliant white. Then two men, Moses and Elijah, began talking with him. They appeared in glorious splendor and spoke about his departure that he was about to carry out at Jerusalem. Now Peter and those with him were quite sleepy, but as they became fully awake they saw his glory and the two men standing with him. Then as the men were starting to leave, Peter said to Jesus, "Master, it is good for us to be here. Let us make three shelters, one for you and one for Moses and one for Elijah"–not knowing what he was saying. As he was saying this, a cloud came and overshadowed them, and they were afraid as they entered the cloud. Then a voice came from the cloud, saying, "This is my Son, my Chosen One. Listen to him!"
	Hebrews 1:4–5; 5:5–6 (Net Bible) Jesus' Exaltation: Thus he (= Jesus) became so far better than the angels as he has inherited a name superior to theirs. For to which of the angels did God ever say, "*You are my son! Today I have fathered you*"? And in another place he says, "*I will be his father and he will be my son.*" So also Christ did not glorify himself in becoming high priest, but the one who glorified him was God, who said to him, "*You are my Son! Today I have fathered you,*" as also in another place God says, "*You are a priest forever in the order of Melchizedek.*"

Jesus recognized that he was the Davidic king of promise	**Mark 8:27–39** (NET Bible) Jesus' Acceptance of Peter's Confession: Then Jesus and his disciples went to the villages of Caesarea Philippi. On the way he asked his disciples, "Who do people say that I am?" They said, "John the Baptist, others say Elijah, and still others, one of the prophets." He asked them, "But who do you say that I am?" Peter answered him, "You are the Christ." Then he warned them not to tell anyone about him.

Mark 14:53, 57–62 (NET Bible)

Jesus Trial before the High Priest: Then they led Jesus to the high priest, and all the chief priests and elders and experts in the law came together.

Some stood up and gave this false testimony against him: "We heard him say, 'I will destroy this temple made with hands and in three days build another not made with hands.'" Yet even on this point their testimony did not agree. Then the high priest stood up before them and asked Jesus, "Have you no answer? What is this that they are testifying against you?" But he was silent and did not answer. Again the high priest questioned him, "Are you the Christ, the Son of the Blessed One?" "I am," said Jesus, "and you will see *the Son of Man sitting at the right hand* of the Power and *coming with the clouds of heaven.*"

Peter and Paul preached that Jesus was the Davidic king of promise	**Acts 2:29–36** (NET Bible) Peter preached: "Brothers, I can speak confidently to you about our forefather David, that he both died and was buried, and his tomb is with us to this day. So then, because he was a prophet and knew that God *had sworn to him with an oath to seat one of his descendants on his throne*, David by foreseeing this spoke about the resurrection of the Christ, that *he was neither abandoned to Hades*, nor did his body *experience decay*. This Jesus God raised up, and we are all witnesses of it. So then, exalted to the right hand of God, and having received the promise of the Holy Spirit from the Father, he has poured out what you both see and hear. For David did not ascend into heaven, but he himself says, '***The Lord said to my lord, "Sit at my right hand until I make your enemies a footstool for your feet."***' Therefore let all the house of Israel know beyond a doubt that God has made this Jesus whom you crucified both Lord and Christ."

Acts 13:32–33, 36–38 (NET Bible)

Paul preached: "And we proclaim to you the good news about the promise to our ancestors, that this promise God has fulfilled to us, their children, by raising Jesus, as also it is written in the second psalm, '***You are my Son today I have fathered you.***'

For David, after he had served God's purpose in his own generation, died, was buried with his ancestors, and experienced decay, but the one whom God raised up did not experience decay. Therefore let it be known to you, brothers, that through this one forgiveness of sins is proclaimed to you, and by this one everyone who believes is justified from everything from which the law of Moses could not justify you.

An _____ announced to Mary that Jesus would be the coming Davidic

Messiah of promise, _____ proclaimed Jesus to be the Davidic Messiah of

promise, _____ recognized that he was the Davidic King of promise and preached about God's Kingdom, and later _____ preached of Jesus fulfilling

God's promise to David.

For Further Reading: Although Solomon was viewed as the initial royal priest of promise who set into motion God's promise to David (1 Kings 1:30, 38–40, 48; cf. Psalm 110), the ultimate king of promise is Jesus who is a divine royal priest far greater than Solomon (Hebrews 1:1–13; cf. Matthew 12:42b). The recognition of Jesus as "Christ" is in keeping with other New Testament texts where Jesus says he came as Messiah to usher in God's kingdom (Mark 1:14–15; cf. Matt. 2:2–11, 4:17; Luke 4:43–44; 10:9–11). The symbolism of Jesus sitting at God's right hand is not unique to Jesus. Similar symbolism is used of a king's honored position and divine right to rule over Israel (Psalms 2, 72, 110; cf. 1 Chronicles 17:4, 28:5; 2 Chronicles 9:8, 13:8). Whereas Yahweh was literally enthroned in heaven (Psalms 2:4, 9:7, 29:10; Isaiah 6:1), the depiction of a Davidic king sitting at Yahweh's right hand in Hebrew Scriptures served as a symbol of honor and right to rule (Psalms 80:17, 89:21). Elsewhere in the New Testament, the literal presence of Jesus in heaven at God's right hand describes his honored position with God and authority to rule as royal priest (cf. Acts 2:24–33, 5:31, 7:55–56; Ephesians 1:20–21; Colossians 3:1; Hebrews 1:3, 8–9; 2:8; 5:9–10) and currently rules over an invisible kingdom (Hebrews 12:22–23; 2 Peter 1:11). God thereby has blessed David's royal line through Jesus and has inaugurated the Davidic covenant. In fact, to deny that Jesus is Messiah is to deny having a relationship with God (1 John 2:22–23; 5:1; cf. 2 John v.7; Jude v.4).

C. _____ _____ God's promise of a new covenant.

Luke 22:14–20 (NET Bible)

Now when the hour came, Jesus took his place at the table and the apostles joined him. And he said to them, "I have earnestly desired to eat this Passover with you before I suffer. For I tell you, I will not eat it again until it is fulfilled in the kingdom of God." Then he took a cup, and after giving thanks he said, "Take this and divide it among yourselves. For I tell you that from now on I will not drink of the fruit of the vine until the kingdom of God comes." Then he took bread, and after giving thanks he broke it and gave it to them, saying, "This is my body which is given for you. Do this in remembrance of me." And in the same way he took the cup after they had eaten, saying, "This cup that is poured out for you is the new covenant in my blood.

Hebrews 10:1–4; 10–18 (NET Bible)

For the law possesses a shadow of the good things to come but not the reality itself, and is therefore completely unable, by the same sacrifices offered continually, year after year, to perfect those who come to worship. For otherwise would they not have ceased to be offered, since the worshipers would have been purified once for all and so have no further consciousness of sin? But in those sacrifices there is a reminder of sins year after year. For the blood of bulls and goats cannot take away sins.

By his (= God's) will we have been made holy through the offering of the body of Jesus Christ once for all. And every priest stands day after day serving and offering the same sacrifices again and again—sacrifices that can never take away sins. But when this priest (= Jesus) had offered one sacrifice for sins for all time, *he sat down at the right hand* of God, where he is now waiting *until his enemies are made a footstool for his feet.* For by one offering he has perfected for all time those who are made holy. And the Holy Spirit also witnesses to us, for after saying, "*This is the covenant that I will establish with them after those days, says the Lord. I will put my laws on their hearts and I will inscribe them on their minds,*" then he says, "*Their sins and their lawless deeds I will remember no longer.*" Now where there is forgiveness of these, there is no longer any offering for sin.

During his earthly ministry Jesus experienced human suffering and death (= spilled his

blood), which served as the means by which God inaugurated the new covenant whereby people who trust that Jesus is the one through whom God fulfilled his promises can experience God's _____, can gain God's _____ (= the internalization of God's expectations for right living), and can expect _____ to eternal life.

For Further Reading: The new covenant is also evident in 1 Corinthians 11:25 and 2 Corinthians 3:6. By means of the new covenant promises, God (through King Jesus) lavishes spiritual blessings upon believers (Ephesians 1:3; Titus 3:4–7). All believers have an enduring relationship with God as "his people" (Romans 9:24–29), are part of God's new creation (2 Corinthians 5:17; Galatians 6:15; cf. 2 Corinthians 4:16; Ephesians 4:23–24; Colossians 3:10), are oriented to God through a "new heart" (Romans 5:5; Galatians 4:6; cf. Acts 2:16, 11:1–18; Ephesians 1:13) and thereby a lifestyle of obedience (John 16:12–15; Romans 6:17–18, 22; 1 Corinthians 2:9–16), are forgiven (Romans 3:22–26; Ephesians 1:7; Colossians 1:14), and are resurrected (Ephesians 2:6).

Point 3 Summarized: Jesus, who is the ultimate descendant of Abraham and the ultimate promised king, inaugurated through the shedding of his blood not only the new covenant but also God's entire kingdom-redemption program.

IV. GOD'S STORY CONCLUDES WITH _____

A. Jesus will _____.

Jesus' return generates anticipation	**Acts 1:3–11** (NET Bible)
	To the same apostles also, after his suffering, he presented himself alive with many convincing proofs. He was seen by them over a forty-day period and spoke about matters concerning the kingdom of God. While he was with them, he declared, "Do not leave Jerusalem, but wait there for what my Father promised, which you heard about from me. For John baptized with water, but you will be baptized with the Holy Spirit not many days from now."
	So when they had gathered together, they began to ask him, "Lord, is this the time when you are restoring the kingdom to Israel?" He told them, "You are not permitted to know the times or periods that the Father has set by his own authority. But you will receive power when the Holy Spirit has come upon you, and you will be my witnesses in Jerusalem, and in all Judea and Samaria, and to the farthest parts of the earth." After he had said this, while they were watching, he was lifted up and a cloud hid him from their sight. As they were still staring into the sky while he was going, suddenly two men in white clothing stood near them and said, "Men of Galilee, why do you stand here looking up into the sky? This same Jesus who has been taken up from you into heaven will come back in the same way you saw him go into heaven."
Anticipation of Jesus' return influences emotions	**1 Thessalonians 4:13–18** (NET Bible)
	Now we do not want you to be uninformed, brothers and sisters, about those who are asleep, so that *you will not grieve like the rest* who have no hope. For if we believe that Jesus died and rose again, so also we believe that God will bring with him those who have fallen asleep as

Christians. For we tell you this by the word of the Lord, that we who are alive, who are left until the coming of the Lord, will surely not go ahead of those who have fallen asleep. For the Lord himself will come down from heaven with a shout of command, with the voice of the archangel, and with the trumpet of God, and the dead in Christ will rise first. Then we who are alive, who are left, will be suddenly caught up together with them in the clouds to meet the Lord in the air. And so we will always be with the Lord. Therefore encourage one another with these words.

Anticipation of Jesus' return shapes conduct

Titus 2:11–13 (Net Bible)

For the grace of God has appeared, bringing salvation to all people. It trains us to **reject godless ways** and worldly desires and to live self-controlled, upright, and godly lives in the present age, as we wait for the happy fulfillment of our hope in the glorious appearing of our great God and Savior, Jesus, *who is the* Christ. He gave himself for us to set us free from every kind of lawlessness and to purify for himself a people who are truly his, who are eager to do good.

Anticipation of Jesus' return produces staying power

Jude 19–20 (Net Bible)

But you, dear friends, by building yourselves up in your most holy faith, by praying in the Holy Spirit, **maintain yourselves in the love of God**, while anticipating the mercy of our Lord Jesus Christ that brings eternal life.

Followers of Jesus can expect that Jesus our Messiah will return, which in turn *affects* our

_____, *shapes* our _____, and *produces* _____ power.

B. Jesus will _____ and _____.

John 16:8–11 (NET Bible)

And when he (= Jesus) comes, he will prove the world wrong concerning sin and righteousness and judgment– concerning sin, because they do not believe in me; concerning righteousness, because I am going to the Father and you will see me no longer; and concerning judgment, because the ruler of this world has been condemned.is the new covenant in my blood.

Jude 14–15 (NET Bible)

Now Enoch, the seventh in descent beginning with Adam, even prophesied of them, saying, "Look! The Lord (= Jesus) is coming with thousands and thousands of his holy ones, to execute judgment on all, and to convict every person of all their thoroughly ungodly deeds that they have committed, and of all the harsh words that ungodly sinners have spoken against him."

For Further Reading: Although Jesus comes, judges, and condemns, he does so in light of God the Father's directive (John 5:22, 26–27, 30). Jesus recognized that he does not judge alone, but that he will judge together with God the Father (John 8:16). Though the details of Jesus coming as judge remain sketchy, we need not worry and get so dogmatic about it. What God wants from us is to trust him and leave the details to him.

C. Jesus will establish God's _____ on earth.

1. _____- Millennial View: Spiritual, Physical, and Eternal

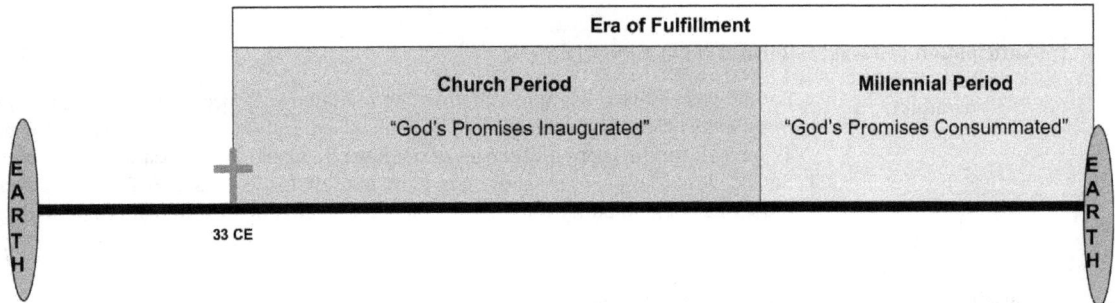

2. _____Millennial View: Spiritual and Eternal

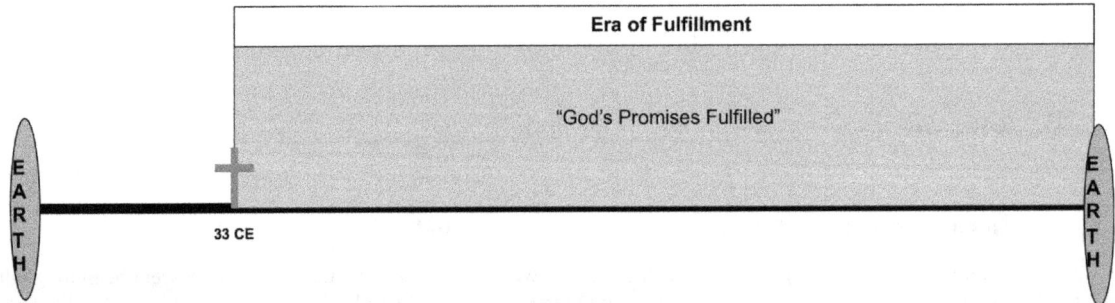

Colossians 1:13–14 (NET Bible)	Revelation 1:5–6 (NET Bible)	1 Corinthians 15:22–24 (NET Bible)
He delivered us from the power of darkness and transferred us to the *kingdom of the Son* he loves, in whom we have redemption, the forgiveness of sins.	To the one (= Jesus) who loves us and has set us free from our sins at the cost of his own blood and *has appointed us as a kingdom*, as priests serving his God and Father—to him be the glory and the power for ever and ever! Amen.	For just as in Adam all die, so also in Christ all will be made alive. But each in his own order: Christ, the firstfruits; then when Christ comes, those who belong to him. Then comes the end, when he hands over the kingdom to God the Father, when he has brought to an end all rule and all authority and power.

For Further Reading: For passages supporting a millennial view see Acts 1:6 where his disciples are still expecting the restoration of Israel. Jesus also spoke of end time events and how when they are seen believers will know that *"the kingdom of God is near"* (Luke 21:31). Thus it appears as though Jesus' royal rule on earth over a restored national Israel has yet to occur. Abraham looked forward to a physical-earthly city (Hebrews 11:10) and followers of Jesus continue to look forward to a city yet to come (Hebrews 13:14; cf. Acts 1:6–8) from where Jesus will rule as king over the earth. Consequently, the consummated kingdom will be God's promised kingdom (James 2:5) that is unshakable (Hebrews 12:28) and eternal (2 Peter 1:11).

Point 4 Summarized: Jesus, who is the ultimate descendant of Abraham and the ultimate promised king who distributed new covenant blessings will come again, will judge all people, and will hand over to God the kingdom and the redeemed people of the kingdom (= new creation).

CONCLUSION

Despite the opening disruption (= disobedience) of God's desire for creation and relationship with the people he created, our eternal king set into motion a plan to restore his _____ rule on earth and _____ a people to enter into that kingdom; a plan that pointed us to, prepared us for, and ends with _____, _____ and a new creation and rulership.

David M. Howard Jr. (PhD, University of Michigan) is dean of the Center for Biblical and Theological Foundations and professor of Old Testament at Bethel Seminary. He has published five books and numerous journal articles, book chapters, and essays.

Interpreting the Pentateuch:
An Exegetical Handbook
Peter T. Vogt
978-0-8254-2762-6 • Paperback • 224 pages • $21.99

Interpreting the Historical Books:
An Exegetical Handbook
Robert B. Chisholm
978-0-8254-2764-0 • Paperback • 232 pages • $19.99

Interpreting the Psalms:
An Exegetical Handbook
Mark D. Futato
978-0-8254-2765-7 • Paperback • 240 pages • $20.99

Interpreting the Prophetic Books:
An Exegetical Handbook
Gary V. Smith
978-0-8254-4363-3 • Paperback • 224 pages • $22.99

John D. Harvey (PhD, Wycliffe College, University of Toronto) is Professor of New Testament and Dean of the Seminary & School of Ministry at Columbia International University. Harvey is the author of *Listening to the Text: Oral Patterning in Paul's Letters, Greek Is Good Grief: Laying the Foundation for Exegesis and Exposition*, and *Anointed with the Spirit and Power: A Biblical Theology of Holy Spirit Empowerment*.

Interpreting the General Letters:
An Exegetical Handbook
Herbert W. Bateman IV
978-0-8254-2768-8 • Paperback • 320 pages • $29.99

Interpreting the Pauline Letters:
An Exegetical Handbook
John D. Harvey
978-0-8254-2767-1 • Paperback • 224 pages • $22.99

Kregel Academic • Rights: World

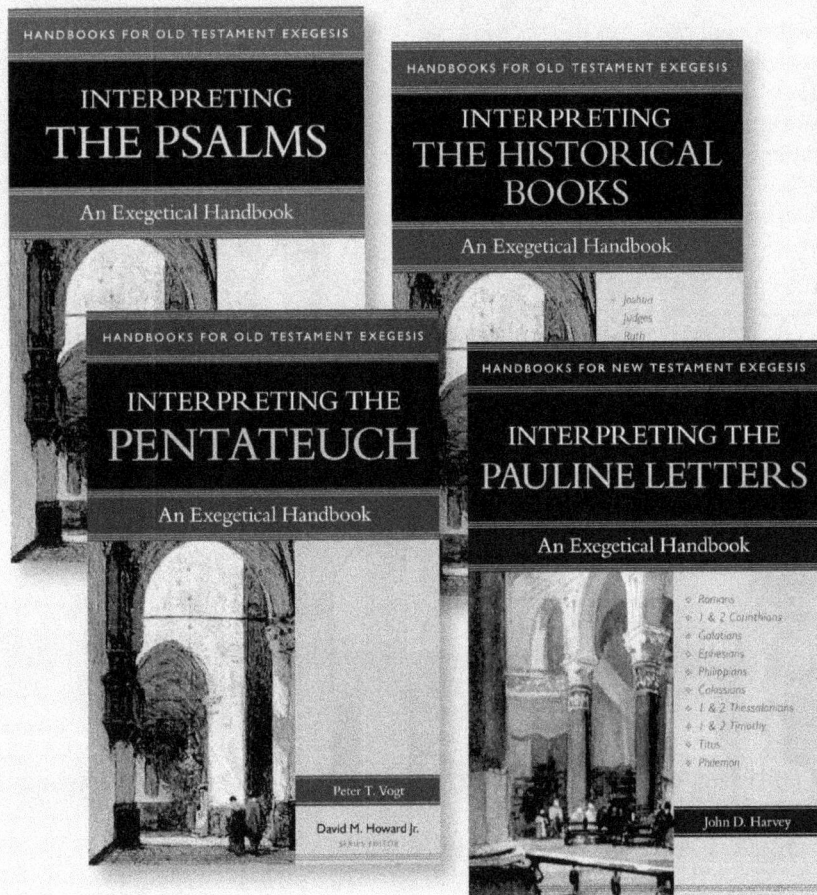

Handbooks for Old Testament Exegesis
David M. Howard Jr., series editor

The Old Testament displays a remarkable literary and theological unity through a variety of genres. But applying a single, one-size-fits-all method of exegesis can lead to confusion and misunderstanding. A valuable reference tool for students and pastors, the Handbooks for Old Testament Exegesis (HOTE) series provides readers with an enhanced understanding of different Old Testament genres and strategies for interpretation.

Forthcoming Handbooks include:
Interpreting the Wisdom Literature Richard L. Schultz

Handbooks for New Testament Exegesis
John D. Harvey, series editor

The Handbooks for New Testament Exegesis (HNTE) series provides readers with an enhanced understanding of different New Testament genres and strategies for interpretation, following in the footsteps of the well-received Handbooks for Old Testament Exegesis series.

Forthcoming Handbooks include:
Interpreting the Gospels and Acts David L. Turner

GOD'S PAST STORY

by Timothy D. Sprankle

I. THE BOOK OF GENESIS

A. What is the subject of Genesis?

Genesis is a book about the _____ of the people of God.

– First people: Adam & Eve

– First place: Eden

– First problem: Rebellion

– First solution: Ark & Abraham

B. What is the occasion and why does Moses write the book of Genesis?

1. What is the occasion for Genesis?

Moses wrote _____ to show the _____ generation

about their unique place in the plan and purpose of God.

CHART 2.1: Representative List of References for Mosaic Authorship (NET Bible)	
Exodus 15:1	Then Moses and the Israelites sang this song to the Lord…
Exodus 24:4	and Moses wrote down all the words of the Lord…
Deuteronomy 31:9, 18	Then Moses wrote down this law and gave it to the Levitical priests, who carry the ark of the Lord's covenant, and to all Israel's elders… So on that day Moses wrote down this song and taught it to the Israelites…
John 1:45	Philip found Nathanael and told him, "We have found the one Moses wrote about in the law, and the prophets also wrote about—Jesus of Nazareth, the son of Joseph."
Acts 7:22	So Moses was trained in all the wisdom of the Egyptians and was powerful in his words and deeds.
"law of Moses"	Joshua 8:31-32; 23:6; 1 Kings 2:3; 2 Kings 14:5; 23:25; 2 Chronicles 23:18; 30:16; Ezra 3:2; 7:6; Nehemiah 8:1; Daniel 9:11, 13; Malachi 4:4; Luke 2:22; 24:44; John 7:23; Acts 13:39; 15:5; 28:23; 1 Corinthians 9:9; Hebrews 10:28

2. **Why did Moses write the book of Genesis?**

Moses fought against the _____ worldview of Ancient Near Eastern

peoples; he counteracts Egyptian and Canaanite mythology with a history of Israel's

beginnings.

CHART 2.2: Comparisons with Ancient Near Eastern Literature		
Country /Date*	Key Document	Key Differences in Genesis
Babylon (20th BC)	**Enuma Elish** – Several gods populate the heavens with their offspring, whom prove troubling. The younger gods revolt. Their leader Marduk creates the world from their mother's corpse. Babylon becomes Marduk's dwelling place, built by humans made from the blood of slain gods.	**Regarding Creation...** One God God speaks creation into existence God is separate from creation God is sovereign over creation
Egypt (24th BC)	**Miscellaneous myths** – Diverse creation myths name different gods (e.g., Re, Ptah) who conquer chaos, spawn other gods, and spin the world into order, separating its elements and naming them.	**Regarding Humanity...** Humanity bears God's image, but separate from God. Humanity is God's vice-regent Humanity is not God's slaves. Humanity cannot win immortality.
Mesopotamia (17th BC)	**Story of Atrahasis** – A story of three gods who created the world, fought, and eventually subjected humanity to slavery. Eventually one god sends a flood to destroy humanity. Atrahasis, a mortal who catches wind of the plot, escapes the flood in a boat.	**Regarding Flood...** Flood a direct consequence of sin. God makes escape possible – ark God makes covenant with creation following the flood.
Sumeria (20th BC) *Dates are approximations	**Gilgamesh Epic** – The titled hero seeks eternal life. On his quest, he must survive a massive flood sent by the gods. He loads the boat with animals until the waters subside.	"Genesis 1 sits in stark contrast to that dark mythological polytheism [of ANE]. The biblical account has as its chief purpose to glorify the one Creator God..." (Courdain, *Against the Gods*, 46)

For further reading: See the various ways Israel retells her Creation Story in these biblical texts: Job 38-40; Psalm 8; 19:1-6; 104; Proverbs 8:22-31; Isaiah 40:12-31; John 1:1-14; Revelation 21:1-5. For a great primer on Ancient Near Eastern [ANE] cosmology, read Courdain, *Against the Gods: The Polemical Theology of the Old Testament* (Wheaton, IL: Crossway, 2013).

C. What is Moses's message to the people of God wandering in the wilderness?

Moses traces Israel's family history back to her earliest beginnings so that the people of

God understand His _____ creation, sin's devastating consequences, and God's

_____ work of redemption through the _____ with Abram.

D. A key verse for understanding Moses' message is found in _____.

Now the Lord said to Abram, "Go out from your country, your relatives, and your father's household to the land that I will show you. Then I will make you into a great nation, and I will bless you, and I will make your name great, so that you will exemplify divine blessing. I will bless those who bless you, but the one who treats you lightly I must curse, and all the families of the earth will bless one another by your name." (NET Bible)

Genesis 15:13-16 (NET Bible)

Then the Lord said to Abram, "Know for certain that your descendants will be strangers in a foreign country. They will be enslaved and oppressed for four hundred years. But I will execute judgment on the nation that they will serve. Afterward they will come out with many possessions. But as for you, you will go to your ancestors in peace and be buried at a good old age. In the fourth generation your descendants will return here, for the sin of the Amorites has not yet reached its limit."

- Abram **believes** and God counts him righteous
- **Covenant** cut/consumed
- **Exile** and return **to land**
- 400 years time period
- Sin of Amorites

Genesis 17:3-8 (NET Bible)

No longer will your name be Abram. Instead, your name will be Abraham because I will make you the father of a multitude of nations. I will make you extremely fruitful. I will make nations of you, and kings will descend from you. I will confirm my covenant as a perpetual covenant between me and you. It will extend to your descendants after you throughout their generations. I will be your God and the God of your descendants after you. I will give the whole land of Canaan—the land where you are now residing—to you and your descendants after you as a permanent possession. I will be their God."

- God changes Abram's **name**
- **Circumcision** is a covenant sign
- God predicts **royalty** in Abraham's line

Genesis 22:15-18 (NET Bible)

"'I solemnly swear by my own name,' decrees the Lord, 'that because you have done this and have not withheld your son, your only son, I will indeed bless you, and I will greatly multiply your descendants so that they will be as countless as the stars in the sky or the grains of sand on the seashore. Your descendants will take possession of the strongholds of their enemies. Because you have obeyed me, all the nations of the earth will pronounce blessings on one another using the name of your descendants.'"

- Abraham **offers** Isaac
- God provides a ram
- God swears an **oath** to confirm his promise
- Blessing to nations reiterated

CHART 2.4: Key Words in Genesis and Their References	
Bless, blessed, blessing Hebrew *barak,* **barakoth**	1:22, 28; 2:3; 5:2; 9:1, 26; 12:2-3 (5x); 14:19-20 (3x); 17:16, 20; 18:18; 22:17-18; 24:1; 24:27, 31, 35, 48, 60; 25:11; 26:3-4 , 12, 24, 29; 27:4, 7, 10, **12**, 19, 23, 25, 27 (2x), 29 (2x), 30, 31, 33 (2x), 34, **35**, **36 (2x)**, **38** (2x), **41** (2x); 28:1, 3, **4**; 6 (2x), 14; 30:27, 30; 31:55; 32:26, 29; **33:11**; 35:9; **39:5** (2x); 47:7, 10; 48:3, 9, 15, 16, 20 (2x); **49:25-26** (6x); **49:28** (3x) <div align="right">**Total 86x**</div>
Curse, cursed, despised Hebrew *arar,* **qalal**	3:14, 17; 4:11; 5:29; **8:21**; 9:25; 12:3 (2x); **16:5**; **27:12-13**, 29; 49:7 <div align="right">**Total 13x**</div>
Good, fine, beautiful Hebrew *tob,* **yatab** (verb)	1:4, 10, 12, 18, 21, 25, 31; 2:9 (2x), 12, 17, 18; 3:5, 6, 22; **4:7**; 6:2; **12:13, 16**; 15:15; 16:6; 18:7; 19:8; 20:15; 24:10, 16; 50; 25:8; 26:7, 29; 27:9, 46; 29:19; 30:20; 31:24, 29; **32:10, 13; 34:18; 40:14**, 16; 41:5, 22, 24, 26 (2x), 35, **37**; 44:4; **45:16**, 18, 20, 23; 49:15; 50:20 <div align="right">**Total 55x**</div>
Evil, bad, ugly, distress Hebrew *ra,* **raah**	2:9, 17; 3:5, 22; **6:5** (2x); 8:21; 13:13; **19:19**; 24:50; **26:29**; 28:8; 31:24, 29, **52**; **37:20, 33**; 38:7; **39:9**; 40:7; 41:3, 11, 19-21 (4x), 27; 43:33; **44:4, 29**; 47:9; 48:16; **50:15, 17, 20** <div align="right">**Total 35x**</div>
Multiply, be great; *Multitude, many, much* Hebrew *rabah* (verb), **rob**	1:22 (2x), 28; 3:16; 6:1, **5**; 7:11, **13:6**; **16:10**; 17-18; 8:17; 9:1, 7(2x); 15:1; 16:10; 17:2, 20; **21:34**; 22:17; **24:25**; **25:23**; 26:4, **14**, 24; **27:28**; 28:3; **30:30, 43; 32:13; 33:9**; 34:12; 35:11; **36:7**; **37:34**; 41:49; 43:34; **45:28**; 47:27; 48:4, **16, 19; 50:20** <div align="right">**Total 44x**</div>

"No leaving, no blessing. Put bluntly, if Abraham had not got up and left for Canaan, the story would have ended right there, or with an endless recycling of the fate of Babel. The Bible would be a very thin book indeed" (Wright, *The Mission of God*, 206).

E. The literary flow of Genesis

PRIMEVAL HISTORY: **Creation and Fall** (1-11)

_____ of Eden, Eikos, and Everything Else (1:1-2:24)

_____ of Humankind and Curse on Creation (3:1-30)

_____ of Humankind: from Fratricide to Babel (4:1-11:26)

PATRIARCHAL HISTORY: **Covenant** (12-50)

Abraham _____ and Confirmed as Father of Promise (11:27-25:11)

Jacob _____ and Bearer of the Birthright (25:19-35:29)

Joseph Exiled and _____ as Steward in Egypt (37:2-36; 39:1-50:26)

Abraham's Other Offspring – _____ (25:12-18)

Isaac's Other Offspring – _____ (36:1-37:1)

Jacob's Other Offspring – _____ (38:1-26; 49:8-12)

For further reading: Trace the various "records [of the generations]" (*toledoth*) of family lines in Genesis, which act as literary markers throughout the book (2:4; 5:1; 6:9; 10:1, 32; 11:10, 27; 25:12; 25:19; 36:1, 9; 37:2).

F. Particulars about Genesis for grasping God's Big Picture

1. GOD'S CREATIVE INTENT

a.	Goodness of Creation	"God said, 'Let there be… God saw that [it] was good." (Genesis 1:4, 10, 12, 18, 21, 25, 31; NET Bible)
b.	Dignity of Humanity	Then God said, "Let us make humankind in our image, after our likeness, so they may rule over the fish of the sea and the birds of the air, over the cattle, and over all the earth, and over all the creatures that move on the earth." God created humankind in his own image, in the image of God he created them, male and female he created them. God blessed them and said to them, "Be fruitful and multiply! Fill the earth and subdue it! Rule over the fish of the sea and the birds of the air and every creature that moves on the ground." (Genesis 1:26-28; NET Bible)

2. OUR REBELLIOUS BENT

Gravitational Pull of Disobedience	"But if you do not do what is right, sin is crouching at the door. It desires to dominate you, but you must subdue it." (Genesis 4:7; NET Bible)

"But the Lord saw the wickedness of humankind had become great on the earth. Every inclination of the thoughts of their minds was only evil all the time." (Genesis 6:5; NET Bible) |

3. GOD'S ENDURING GOOD

Blessing of Forgiveness	When Joseph's brothers saw that their father was dead, they said, "What if Joseph bears a grudge and wants to repay us in full for all the harm we did to him?" So they sent word to Joseph, saying, "Your father gave these instructions before he died: 'Tell Joseph this: Please forgive the sin of your brothers and the wrong they did when they treated you so badly.' Now please forgive the sin of the servants of the God of your father." When this message was reported to him, Joseph wept. Then his brothers also came and threw themselves down before him; they said, "Here we are; we are your slaves." But Joseph answered them, "Don't be afraid. Am I in the place of God? As for you, you meant to harm me, but God intended it for a good purpose, so he could preserve the lives of many people, as you can see this day. So now, don't be afraid. I will provide for you and your little children." Then he consoled them and spoke kindly to them. (Genesis 50:15-21; NET Bible)

"In Genesis, Yahweh's grace is bound up extensively with his sovereignty. As we have seen, Genesis 50:20 highlights Yahweh's sovereignty, as Joseph notes God was able to turn the evil inclinations of his brothers into good, so that the people were persevered alive. By exercising his sovereignty, God graciously blesses his people and preserves them. Moreover, this grace extends, not only to the Israelites, but also the Egyptians, who benefit from Joseph's wise, godly leadership…" (Vogt, *Interpreting the Pentateuch*, 80).

II.   THE MESSAGE OF 1–2 SAMUEL

A. What is the subject of 1 and 2 Samuel?

The subject of 1–2 Samuel is _____ for the people of God.

Predictions of a King in Scripture:

- Genesis 17:6 – Abraham's line
- Genesis 49:10 – Judah's line
- Numbers 24:17 – Balaam's oracle
- Deuteronomy 17:14-20 – Mosaic Law
- Judges 8:22-23 – Israel's offer to Gideon
- 1 Samuel 2:10 – Hannah's song

CHART 3.1: A King Predicted by God's People	
Genesis 17:6 (NET Bible)	I will make you extremely fruitful. I will make nations of you, and kings will descend from you.
Genesis 49:10 (NET Bible)	The scepter will not depart from Judah, nor the ruler's staff from between his feet, until he comes to whom it belongs; the nations will obey him.
Numbers 24:17 (NET Bible)	'A star will march forth out of Jacob, and a scepter will rise out of Israel.'
Deuteronomy 17:14-20 (NET Bible)	When you come to the land the Lord your God is giving you and take it over and live in it and then say, "I will select a king like all the nations surrounding me," you must select without fail a king whom the Lord your God chooses. From among your fellow citizens you must appoint a king—you may not designate a foreigner who is not one of your fellow Israelites. Moreover, he must not accumulate horses for himself or allow the people to return to Egypt to do so, for the Lord has said you must never again return that way. Furthermore, he must not marry many wives lest his affections turn aside, and he must not accumulate much silver and gold. When he sits on his royal throne he must make a copy of this law on a scroll given to him by the Levitical priests. It must be with him constantly and he must read it as long as he lives, so that he may learn to revere the Lord his God and observe all the words of this law and these statutes and carry them out. Then he will not exalt himself above his fellow citizens or turn from the commandments to the right or left, and he and his descendants will enjoy many years ruling over his kingdom in Israel.

| Judges 8:22-23 (NET Bible) | The men of Israel said to Gideon, "Rule over us—you, your son, and your grandson. For you have delivered us from Midian's power." Gideon said to them, "I will not rule over you, nor will my son rule over you. The Lord will rule over you." |
| 1 Samuel 2:10 (NET Bible) | The Lord shatters his adversaries; he thunders against them from the heavens. The Lord executes judgment to the ends of the earth. He will strengthen his king, and exalt the power of his anointed one." |

B. What's the occasion? Why does the author write 1-2 Samuel?

1. The authorship and date of 1 and 2 Samuel is _____.

2. The final form of 1 and 2 Samuel was reached after _____ monarchy.

3. Written to trace the monarchy to its roots and highlight its ideal King, David

Summation of the Occasion for 1 and 2 Samuel: While authorship and date are uncertain (see 1 Chronicles 29:29-30), 1 and 2 Samuel reached its final form after the monarchy was divided (931 B.C.). The book traces the monarchy to its roots and highlights its ideal king, David.

For further reading: Examine the following passages from Hebrew Scriptures about a king praised by God's people.

CHART 3.2: A King Praised for God's People	
God's anointed king is inaugurated	Psalm 2, 45, 110
God's anointed king blesses the people	1 Samuel 2:10; Psalm 68, 72, 101
God's anointed king will not be forsaken	Psalm 89, 132
God's anointed king experiences God's deliverance	Psalm 2, 20, 21, 93, 144
Israel's God is King	Psalm 22, 24, 47, 68, 93, 96-99

C. What is the author's message in 1–2 Samuel?

The author of Samuel focuses on God's _____ king, David, so that the

people of God will continue to _____ God's promise for a royal heir

and continue to _____ His word.

CHART 3.3: David's Lineage Traced in the Old Testament							

Salmon	David	Asa	Amaziah	Manasseh			
Boaz	Solomon	Jehoshaphat	Uzziah / Jotham	Amon	Jehoiachin	→→→	Zerubbabel
Jesse	Rehoboam	Jehoram	Ahaz	Josiah	Zedekiah		
	Abijah	Ahaziah	Hezekiah	Jehoahaz			
		Athaliah		Jehoiakim			
cf. Ruth 4:21-22		Joash					cf. Haggai 2:23

1000	900	800	700	600	500	400

Divided Kingdom (931)   Samaria Falls (722)   Jerusalem Falls (587)   (515) Temple Rebuilt

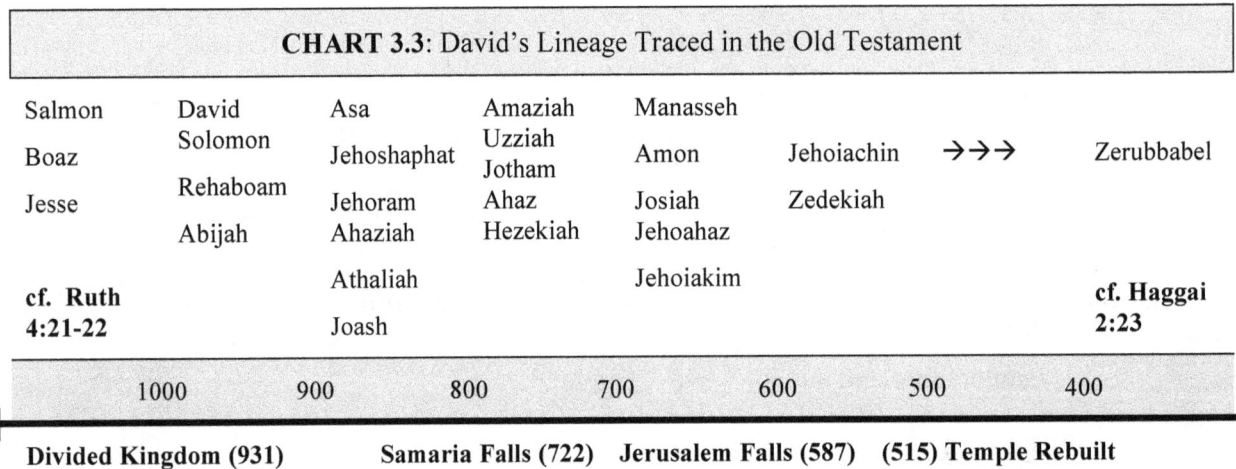

D. A key verse for understanding 1–2 Samuel is found in 2 Samuel _____.

When the time comes for you to die, I will raise up your descendant, one of your own sons, to succeed you, and I will establish his kingdom. He will build a house for my name, and I will make his dynasty permanent. I will become his father and he will become my son. When he sins, I will correct him with the rod of men and with wounds inflicted by human beings. But my loyal love will not be removed from him as I removed it from Saul, whom I removed from before you. Your house and your kingdom will stand before me permanently; your dynasty will be permanent.'" (NET Bible)

CHART 3.4: Tracing Key Words from the Davidic Covenant	
Son	The king says, "I will announce the Lord's decree. He said to me: 'You are my son! This very day I have become your father! (Psalm 2:7; NET Bible cf. Psalm 89:27; 132:11-12; Hebrews 1:1-6)
Kingdom	Your throne, O God, is permanent. The scepter of your kingdom is a scepter of justice. You love justice and hate evil. For this reason God, your God has anointed you with the oil of joy, elevating you above your companions. (Psalm 45:6-7; NET Bible cf. Psalm 89:36-27; 110)
House	Now Moses was *faithful in all God's house* as a servant, to testify to the things that would be spoken. But Christ is faithful as a son over God's house. (Hebrews 3:5-6a, NET Bible)
Loyal Love	I will sing continually about the Lord's faithful deeds; to future generations I will proclaim your faithfulness. For I say, "Loyal love is permanently established; in the skies you set up your faithfulness." The Lord said, "I have made a covenant with my chosen one;

> I have made a promise on oath to David, my servant:
> "I will give you an eternal dynasty
> and establish your throne throughout future generations.'"
>
> I will always extend my loyal love to him,
> and my covenant with him is secure.
>
> But I will not remove my loyal love from him,
> nor be unfaithful to my promise.
>
> (Psalm 89:1-3, 28, 33; NET Bible cf. Exodus 34:5-7; Psalm 86:15; 145:8; 103:4, 8, 11, 17)

For further reading: Note how King David knows God keeps his promise to David's royal heir in 2 Samuel 23:1-7 and 1 Kings 1:1-2:12. Consider the importance of Solomon's Temple and its dedication in light of the promise to David in 1 Kings 8-9.

E. The Literary Flow of 1-2 Samuel

1. The Prophetic Ministry of Samuel (1 Samuel 1-15)

2. The Conflicted Kingdom of Saul (1 Samuel 16-31)

3. The Enduring Kingdom of David (2 Samuel 1-20)

4. Reflections on King David (2 Samuel 21-24)

F. Particulars for Samuel for grasping God's Big Picture?

1. GOD'S DEMAND FOR OBEDIENCE

Examples of Disobedience

Eli's sons (1 Samuel 2)
Israel and the lost ark (1 Samuel 7)
Samuel's sons (1 Samuel 8)
Saul and illicit sacrifices (1 Samuel 15)
David and Bathsheba (2 Samuel 10)

1 Samuel 15:22 (NET Bible)

"Does the Lord take pleasure in burnt offerings and sacrifices as much as he does in obedience? Certainly, obedience is better than sacrifice; paying attention is better than the fat of rams."

2. MAN'S PROPENSITY TO OPPRESS

Examples of Oppression

Goliath mocks Israel (1 Samuel 17)
Saul hunts David (1 Samuel 18-30)
David kills Uriah (2 Samuel 12)
Ziba cheats Mephibosheth (2 Samuel 16)

Psalm 3:1-2 (NET Bible)

Lord, how numerous are my enemies!
Many attack me. Many say about me,
"God will not deliver him." (Selah)

Rise up, Lord!
Deliver me, my God!
Yes, you will strike all my enemies on the jaw;
you will break the teeth of the wicked.

Facing Oppression

David oppressed by Saul or others
Psalms 3, 7, 18, 34, 52, 53, 56-57, 59, 63, 142

Other psalms of Lament
Psalms 4-6; 10-14; 16-17; 20, 22, 25-28, 31; 35-36; 38-39

The Lord delivers; you show favor to your people. (Selah)

I rested and slept;
I awoke, for the Lord protects me.
I am not afraid of the multitude of people who attack me from all directions.

"Psalms of lament call on God to stop injustice and exploitation and oppression. By calling on God to intervene, the psalmist or the one praying the psalms is affirming that God is the utterly fair and all-knowing Judge. To those suffering, such laments are a message of hope; God will not let the wicked get away with it forever" (Wenham, *The Psalter Reclaimed*, 49).

3. GOD'S DISCERNMENT OF CHARACTER

Examples of Discernment

God hears Hannah's prayer
(1 Samuel 1-2)
God sees David's heart
(1 Samuel 16)

1 Samuel 1:10-16 (NET Bible)

She was very upset as she prayed to the Lord, and she was weeping uncontrollably… Now Hannah was speaking from her heart… "I have poured out my soul to the Lord."

"…Hannah's commitment to the Lord was the catalyst for the revival of genuine Yahweh worship through the spiritual leadership of her son Samuel." (Chisholm, *Interpreting the Historical Books*, 102)

GOD'S CURRENT STORY

by Herbert W. Bateman IV

I. MATTHEW'S GOSPEL MESSAGE

A. Who or what is the subject of Matthew's gospel?

The subject of Matthew's gospel is the presentation and rejection of _____

as God's _____ and coming of God's _____.

B. What is Matthew's occasion for writing? Why does Matthew write his gospel?

We don't know . . . but we surmise from Matthew's content that Matthew is addressing Jewish Christians who are being persecuted by non-believing Jews!

1. Jesus' teaching was in _____ with the religious leaders concerning

living _____.

Matthew 12:5–7 (NET Bible)

Or have you not read in the law that the priests in the temple desecrate the Sabbath and yet are not guilty? I tell you that *something greater than the temple is here*. If you had known what this means: '***I want mercy and not sacrifice***,' you would not have condemned the innocent.

Matthew 17:24–27 (NET Bible)

After they arrived in Capernaum, *the collectors of the temple tax* came to Peter and said, "Your teacher pays the double drachma tax, doesn't he?" He said, "Yes." When Peter came into the house, Jesus spoke to him first, "What do you think, Simon? From whom do earthly kings collect tolls or taxes—from their sons or from foreigners?" After he said, "From foreigners," Jesus said to him, "Then the sons are free. But so that we don't offend them, go to the lake and throw out a hook. Take the first fish that comes up, and when you open its mouth, you will find a four drachma coin. Take that and give it to them for me and you."

Matthew 23:16–22

"Woe to you, blind guides, who say, 'Whoever swears by the temple is bound by nothing. But *whoever swears by the gold of the temple is bound by* the oath.' Blind fools! Which is greater, the gold or the temple that makes the gold sacred? And, 'Whoever swears by the altar is bound by nothing. But if anyone swears by the gift on it he is bound by the oath.' You are blind! For which is greater, the gift or the altar that makes the gift sacred? So whoever swears by the altar swears by it and by everything on it. And *whoever swears by the temple swears by it and the one who dwells in it*. And whoever swears by heaven swears by the throne of God and the one who sits on it.

For Further Reading: The parables (Matthew 21:33–41; 22:2–14) that are directed at the religious leaders evidence the rejection of God's Messiah (= Son) and serve as prime examples of Judean religious leaders' rejection of Jesus. In Matthew 11:16–24, the numerous people who hear Jesus' teaching and see his miracles but do not repent as well as Jesus' denouncement of them is an explicit portrayal of conflict between the people of Judea and Jesus.

2. Jesus as God's promised _____ and his authority was questioned

and in _____ with the expectations of many Judean Jews.

Matthew 1:1–3, 16, 18; 2:1–3 (NET Bible)

This is the record of the genealogy of Jesus, *who is the* Christ, the son of David, the son of Abraham.

Abraham was the father of Isaac, Isaac the father of Jacob, Jacob the father of Judah and his brothers, Judah the father of Perez and Zerah (by Tamar), Perez the father of Hezron, Hezron the father of Ram, . . . , and Jacob the father of Joseph, the husband of Mary, by whom Jesus was born, who is called Christ.

Now the birth of Jesus, *who is the* Christ happened this way. While his mother Mary was engaged to Joseph, but before they came together, she was found to be pregnant through the Holy Spirit.

After Jesus was born in Bethlehem in Judea, in the time of King Herod, wise men from the East came to Jerusalem saying, "Where is the one who is born king of the Jews? For we saw his star when it rose6 and have come to worship him." When King Herod heard this he was alarmed, and all Jerusalem with him.

Matthew 21:7–9, 15 (NET Bible)

They brought the donkey and the colt and placed their cloaks on them, and he sat on them. A very large crowd spread their cloaks on the road. Others cut branches from the trees and spread them on the road. The crowds that went ahead of him and those following kept shouting, "*Hosanna* to the Son of David! ***Blessed is the one who comes in the name of the Lord!*** *Hosanna* in the highest!"

But when the chief priests and the experts in the law saw the wonderful things he did and heard the children crying out in the temple courts, "Hosanna to the Son of David," *they became indignant.*

Matthew 26:26–30 (NET Bible)

While they were eating, Jesus took bread, and after giving thanks he broke it, gave it to his disciples, and said, "Take, eat, this is my body." And after taking the cup and giving thanks, he gave it to them, saying, "Drink from it, all of you, for this is my blood, the blood of the covenant, that is poured out for many for the forgiveness of sins. I tell you, from now on I will not drink of this fruit of the vine until that day when I drink it new with you in my Father's kingdom." After singing a hymn, they went out to the Mount of Olives.

For Further Reading: The "Messiah" emphasis is clear in Matthew from the opening chapters of the book. In 1:1 Jesus is called the "son of David," i.e., "David the King" (1:6). The whole genealogy is structured to show that Jesus is a legitimate descendent of King David and rightful heir to the throne. Frequently, Jesus is addressed as or inferred to be the "Son of David" (9:27; 12:23; 15:22; 20:30–31; 21:9, 15; 22:45). Along similar lines Jesus is presented as the promised "Messiah" (1:16, 17; 2:4; 11:2; 16:16, 20; 22:42; 23:8, 10; 24:5, 23; 26:63,68; 27:17, 22).

The prophecy about the "great ruler" of Israel being born in Bethlehem (Micah 5:2) is applied to Jesus (2:6). The magi ask Herod, "Where is he who is born King of the Jews?" (2:2). When they find him the magi give gifts suited for a king — gold, frankincense, and myrrh. The transfiguration anticipates Christ coming to his kingdom in glory (16:28; 17:1, 2), which Jesus later reaffirms in the Olivet discourse (24:27–30). Herod the Great, however, sets out to murder the Messiah and so the conflict about Jesus as Messiah begins and progresses throughout Matthew.

Upon Jesus' formal entrance into Jerusalem, Matthew includes a most pointed reference to the royal Messiah in the quote of Zechariah 9:9 "Behold your King is coming to you" (21:5). And, during the passion narrative Jesus is explicitly referred to as "the King of the Jews" three times (27:11, 29, 37) and as "King of Israel" once (27:42). Yet Jesus is brought to trial, condemned, and murdered. The book ends, however, with all authority in heaven and earth being transferred to Jesus (28:18–20; cf. 25:30–46).

3. Matthew presents the repeated offer of the _____ to Judeans, the recurring rejection of God's kingdom (as well as Messiah), and the subsequent _____ of the kingdom to all nations.

Kingdom already present	Kingdom yet to come
Matthew 3:2; 4:14; 10:7; 11:12 (NET Bible)	**Matthew 5:19; 6:10; 7:21; 8:11; 25:1; 13:38–40** (NET Bible)
"Repent, for the kingdom of heaven (= kingdom of God) is near."	So anyone who breaks one of the least of these commands and teaches others to do so will be called least in the kingdom of heaven, but whoever obeys them and teaches others to do so will be called great in the kingdom of heaven (= kingdom of God).
From that time Jesus began to preach this message: "Repent, for the kingdom of heaven (= kingdom of God) is near."	. . . may your kingdom come, may your will be done on earth as it is in heaven.
As you go, preach this message: 'The kingdom of heaven (= kingdom of God) is near!'	"Not everyone who says to me, 'Lord, Lord,' will enter into the kingdom of heaven (= kingdom of God)—only the one who does the will of my Father in heaven.
	I tell you, many will come from the east and west to share the banquet with Abraham, Isaac, and Jacob in the kingdom of heaven (= kingdom of God)
From the days of John the Baptist until now the kingdom of heaven (= kingdom of God) has suffered violence, and forceful people lay hold of it	"At that time the kingdom of heaven (= kingdom of God) will be like ten virgins who took their lamps and went out to meet the bridegroom.
	The field is the world and the good seed are the people of the kingdom. The weeds are the people of the evil one, and the enemy who sows them is the devil. The harvest is the end of the age, and the reapers are angels. As the weeds are collected and burned with fire, so it will be at the end of the age.

Matthew 21:28–31 (NET Bible)
"What do you think? A man had two sons. He went to the first and said, 'Son, go and work in the vineyard today.' The boy answered, 'I will not.' But later he had a change of heart and went. The father went to the other son and said the same thing. This boy answered, 'I will, sir,' but did not go. Which of the two did his father's will?" They said, "The first." Jesus said to them, "I tell you the truth, tax collectors and prostitutes will go ahead of you into the kingdom of God!

For Further Reading: The teachings of Jesus, John, and the apostles are centered on the kingdom of God (3:2; 4:17; 5:3, 10; 10:7). The kingdom of God is to be sought after (6:33) and demands a radical righteousness (5:19–20). Jesus' parables in Matthew 13 are proclamations about God's kingdom and the various responses to the message about the kingdom. Living in God's kingdom requires childlike humility (18:3–4, 10; 19:14), an ability to say I'm sorry (18:15–17), and a willingness to forgive a repentant person (18:23–35). Finally, the kingdom is to be anticipated (25:1–13).

Further Reading: Controversy Stories where Jesus is in Debate with Judeans			
Matthew	**Event**	**Mark**	**Luke**
8:5–13	The Centurion's servant	Not in Mark	7:1–10
9:1–8	The *authority* to forgive sins	2:1–12	5:17–26
9:10–13	Eating with sinners	2:15–17	5:28–32
9:14–17	Fasting	2:18–22	5:33–39
11:2–6	John's Question	Not in Mark	7:18–23
12:1–8	Plucking Grain on the Sabbath	2:23–28	6:1–5
12:9–14	The man with the withered hand	3:1–6	6:6–11
12:22–37	Jesus and Beelzebul	3:22–30	11:14–23
15:1–20	The tradition of the elders	7:1–23	11:37–41
15:21–28	The Syrophoenician woman	7:24–30	Not in Luke
19:3–12	Teachings on divore	10:2–12	Not in Luke
19:16–22	The rich man	10:17–22	18:18–23
20:20–28	The request of James and John	10:35–45	22:24–27
21:23–27	The withered fig tree	11:20–25	Not in Luke
21:23–27	The authority of Jesus	11:27–33	20:1–8
22:15–22	Paying taxes to Caesar	12:13–17	20:20–26
22:23–33	The question about the resurrection	12:18–27	20:27–40
22:34–40	The greatest commandment	12:28–34	10:25–28

Summary Point: So, perhaps Jewish believers were still facing conflict from other Jews and Matthew wrote his gospel to reaffirm Jewish believers that though their teaching about Jesus as Messiah and the presence of the kingdom was in conflict with Jewish teachers of the law, stand firm.

C. What is Matthew's message to the Jewish believers living in Judea?

Matthew's intention for recounting the life, example, and kingdom teachings of Jesus, who is the Messiah, is so that his disciples (= us) might be _____ about Jesus' messiahship and thereby _____ as kingdom saints, _____ the kingdom message, and _____ disciples for the kingdom despite the conflict.

D. What is a key verse for understanding Matthew's Gospel?

Matthew _____

Therefore go and make disciples of all nations, baptizing them in the name of the Father and the Son and the Holy Spirit, teaching them to obey everything I have commanded you. And remember, I am with you always, to the end of the age. (NET Bible)

E. The Literary Flow of Matthew's Gospel Message

Prologue: The Davidic Line of the Messiah, his Birth, and Preservation (1:1–2:23)

  Introduction to Jesus' Messiahship (3:1–4:25)

  Kingdom Teaching about the Kingdom _____ (5:1–7:27)

  Transition: "and it came about when Jesus had finished these words" (7:28-29)

  Display of Jesus' Messiahship in Power and Authority (8:1–11:1)

  Kingdom Teaching about the Kingdom _____ and Potential Suffering (10:5–42)

  Transition: "and it came about when Jesus had finished these instructions" (11:1)

  Examples of Opposition to Jesus' Messiahship (11:2–12:50)

  Kingdom Teaching about the _____ of the Kingdom (13:1–52)

  Transition: "and it came about when Jesus had finished these parables" (13:53)

  Growing Opposition to Jesus' Messiahship and Subsequent Withdraws (13:54–16:12)

  Kingdom Teaching about _____ in the Kingdom (18:1–35)

  Transition: "and it came about when Jesus had finished these words" (19:1–2)

  Formal Presentation of Jesus as Messiah and his Rejection in Jerusalem (19:3–23:39)

  Kingdom Teaching about _____ of the Kingdom (23:1–25:46)

  Transition: "and it came about when Jesus had finished these words" (16:1)

Conclusion: Messiah Jesus is Crucified, Resurrected, and Given all Authority (16:2–28:20)

Summary Point: Matthew's gospel weaves together two complementary themes as the story about Jesus progresses and unfolds.

F. What does Matthew's Gospel contribute to God's big picture?

1. Matthew's narrative material presents Jesus as Messiah and king of Israel, the one through whom God has _____ his promises.

Biblical Texts Cited in Matthew as Fulfillment Citations		
Matthew	**Hebrew Scripture**	**Subject**
1:23	Isaiah 7:14	A virgin will conceive and bear a son called Immanuel.
2:15	Hosea 11:1	God called his Son from Egypt
2:18	Jeremiah 31:15	In Ramah, Rachel mourned her murdered children
2:23	Judges 13:5, 7	The Messiah will be called a Nazarene
4:15–16	Isaiah 9:1–2	Dark Galilee of the Gentiles sees the light
8:17	Isaiah 53:4	The servant bears the nation's diseases
12:18–21	Isaiah 42:1–4	Gentiles will hope in the Spirit-empowered servant
13:35	Psalm 78:2	The psalmist speaks in parables of the deep things
21:5	Isaiah 62:11; Zechariah 9:9	Zion's king appears meekly, riding a donkey's colt
27:9–10	Jeremiah 32:6–9; Zechariah 11:12–13	The purchase of the potter's field for thirty pieces of silver

One Example

Hosea asserts that God loved Israel (God had chosen Israel and was God's firstborn son among the nations) and thereby called the nation Israel from Egypt (= the Exodus).

God had preserved Israel (firstborn son = nation) from the wrath of Pharaoh.

Hosea 11:1–5 (NET Bible)

When Israel was a young man, I loved him like a son, and *I summoned my son out of Egypt*. But the more I summoned them, the farther they departed from me. They sacrificed to the Baal idols and burned incense to images. Yet it was I who led Ephraim, I took them by the arm; but they did not acknowledge that I had healed them. I led them with

Matthew 2:12–15 (NET Bible)

After being warned in a dream not to return to Herod, they (=Magi) went back by another route to their own country. After they (=Magi) had gone, an angel of the Lord appeared to Joseph in a dream and said, "Get up, take the child and his mother and flee to Egypt, and stay there until I tell you, for Herod is going to look for the child to kill him." Then he got up, took the child and his

leather cords, with leather ropes; I lifted the yoke9 from their neck, and gently fed them. They will return to Egypt! Assyria will rule over them because they refuse to repent!

mother during the night, and went to Egypt. He stayed there until Herod24 died. In this way what was spoken by the Lord through the prophet was fulfilled: "*I called my Son out of Egypt*."

> Matthew asserts that God loved Jesus (God had chosen Jesus and was God's firstborn son [king] among the Jewish people) and thereby called Jesus from Egypt.
>
> God had preserved Jesus (firstborn son = king) from the wrath of Herod.

For Further Reading: A favorite phrase throughout Matthew is "This fulfilled what was spoken by the prophet" (1:22; 2:15, 17; 4:14; 8:17; 12:17; 13:35; 21:4; 27:9) or some facsimile (2:23; 3:15; 5:17; 13:48; 23:32; 26:54, 56).

Other Old Testament Citations in Matthew

Matthew's Use of Hebrew Scriptures					
Matthew Reference	Old Testament Quotation	Matthew Reference	Old Testament Quotation	Matthew Reference	Old Testament Quotation
1:23	Isaiah 7:14	9:13	Hosea 6:6	19:19b	Lev 19:18
2:6	Micah 5:2	10:35	Micah 7:6	21:5	Zechariah 9:9
2:15	Hosea 11:1	11:10	Mal. 3:1	21:9	Psalm 118:26
2:18	Jeremiah 31:15		[Exodus 23:20]	21:13a	Isaiah 56:7
3:3	Isaiah 40:3	12:7	Hosea 6:6	21:13b	Jeremiah 7:11
4:4	Deut 8:3	12:18-21	Isaiah 42:1-4	21:16	Psalm 8:2
4:6	Psalm 91:11-12	12:40	Jonah 1:17	21:42	Psalm 118:22-23
4:7	Deut 6:16	13:14-15	Isaiah 6:9-10	22:32	Exodus 3:6
4:10	Deut 6:13	13:35	Psalm 78:2	22:37	Deut 6:5
4:15-16	Isaiah 9:1-2	15:4a	Exodus 20:12	22:39	Lev. 19:18
5:21	Exodus 20:13		Deut 5:16	22:44	Psalm 110:1
	Deut 5:17	15:4b	Exodus 21:17	23:39	Psalm 118:26
5:27	Exodus 20:14		Lev. 20:9	24:15	Daniel 9:27; 11:31
	Deut. 5:18	15:8-9	Isaiah 29:13	24:29	Isaiah 13:10; 34:4
5:31	Deut. 24:1	16:27	Proverbs 24:12	24:30	Daniel 7:13
5:38	Exodus 21:24	17:10-11	Mal. 4:5-6	26:31	Zechariah 13:7
	Lev. 24:20	18:16	Deut 19:15	26:64	Daniel 7:13-14
	Deut. 19:21	19:4	Genesis 1:27; 5:2	27:9-10	Zechariah 11:13
5:43	Lev. 19:18	19:5	Genesis 2:24	27:35	Psalm 22:18
8:17	Isaiah 53:4	19:18-19a	Exodus 20:12-16 Deut 5:16-20	27:46	Psalm 22:1

Summary Point for Matthew's Contribution to God's Big Picture: Matthew's narrative material presents the _____ of the kingdom that are to be _____ with others and _____ out by all who claim to be followers of the king (= Jesus) despite conflict.

II.   PAUL'S LETTER TO THE ROMANS

A. Who or what is the subject of Romans?

The subject of Paul's letter to the Romans is God's _____ .

B. What's the occasion? Why does Paul write to the Romans?

Paul writes to the believers in Rome to prepare the Church for his _____, to

_____ their faith, and to address the current _____

between the Roman Jew and Gentile believers.

Romans 1:8–13 (NET Bible)	**Romans 15:23–29** (NET Bible)
I thank my God through Jesus Christ for all of you, because your faith is proclaimed throughout the whole world. For God, whom I serve in my spirit by preaching the gospel of his Son, is my witness that I continually remember you and I always ask in my prayers, if perhaps now at last I may succeed in visiting you according to the will of God. For I long to see you, so that I may impart to you some spiritual gift to strengthen you, that is, that we may be mutually comforted by one another's faith, both yours and mine. I do not want you to be unaware, brothers and sisters, that I often intended to come to you (and was prevented until now), so that I may have some fruit even among you, just as I already have among the rest of the Gentiles	But now there is nothing more to keep me in these regions, and I have for many years desired to come to you when I go to Spain. For I hope to visit you when I pass through and that you will help me on my journey there, after I have enjoyed your company for a while. But now I go to Jerusalem to minister to the saints. For Macedonia and Achaia are pleased to make some contribution for the poor among the saints in Jerusalem. For they were pleased to do this, and indeed they are indebted to the Jerusalem saints. *For if the Gentiles have shared in their spiritual things, they are obligated also to minister to them in material things*. Therefore after I have completed this and have safely delivered this bounty to them, I will set out for Spain by way of you, and I know that when I come to you I will come in the fullness of Christ's blessing.

For Further Reading: The occasion for writing Romans was to prepare the Christian community for his upcoming visit, which he had been prevented from doing in the past (1:8–15; 15:22–24). Before coming to Rome, Paul reveals that he must go to Jerusalem first with the collection from the churches in Macedonia and Achaia for the poor Christians there (15:25–31; Acts 20:1ff). While on his westward journey to Spain, Paul desires to spend time in Rome so as to be refreshed by their fellowship, interest, and support before continuing on to Spain (15:14–33).

The tension between Jew and Gentile underlies the entire book. In the opening thematic statement Paul declares the gospel to be for both Jew and Gentile (1:16; cf., 2:9–10); both "Jews and Greeks are all under sin" (3:9; cf., 2:14f; 2:17f); since there is only one God, he is the God of the Jew and Gentile alike (3:29); and both come to him through faith (4:1ff).

Furthermore, Gentile inclusion into the promises of God and Jewish rejection are interrelated throughout chapters 9–11. On the one hand, Israel's rejection is not final and they still have the hope of being brought back into the promises. On the other hand, the Gentiles should not get over confident because they are included only because of faith, nothing else. Thus, the two groups are exhorted to live in harmony with one another (14:1ff; particularly in the closing comments of 15:7–13).

C. What is Paul's message to the Christians living in Rome?

Paul's letter to the Romans about God's _____ reveals that

God's righteousness was exercised on behalf all people so that all those who claim to

follow Jesus, namely Messiah, might _____ _____.

Romans 1:1–4 (NET Bible)	Romans 12:1–2 (NET Bible)
From Paul, a slave of Christ Jesus, called to be an apostle, set apart for the gospel of God. This gospel he promised (= to the Jews) beforehand through his prophets in the holy scriptures, concerning his Son who was a descendant of David with reference to the flesh, who was appointed the Son-of-god-in-power according to the Holy Spirit by the resurrection from the dead, Jesus *who is the* Christ our Lord. Through him we have received grace and our apostleship to bring about the obedience of faith among all the Gentiles on behalf of his name. You (= Roman Jew and Gentile believers) also are among them, called to belong to Jesus *who is the* Christ.	Therefore I exhort you, brothers and sisters, by the mercies of God, to present your bodies as a sacrifice—alive, holy, and pleasing to God–which is your reasonable service. Do not be conformed to this present world, but be transformed by the renewing of your mind, so that you may test and approve what is the will of God–what is good and well-pleasing and perfect.

Summary Point: As fellow recipients of God's righteousness available through Jesus who is God's promised and ultimate Davidic king, live righteously.

D. What is a key verse for understanding Paul's message to the Romans?

Romans _____

Thus I am eager also to preach the gospel to you who are in Rome. For I am not ashamed of the gospel, for it is God's power for salvation to everyone who believes, to the Jew first and also to the Greek. For the righteousness of God is revealed in the gospel from faith to faith, just as it is written, '*The righteous by faith will live*.' (NET Bible)

E. The Literary Flow of Paul's Message to the Romans

Prologue (1:1–17)

God's Righteousness _____ in his Universal Plan (1:18–8:39)

Israel's _____ of and Gentile Inclusion in God's Righteousness (9:1–11:36)

Precepts for Righteousness in Everyday _____ (12:1–15:13)

Epilogue (15:14–16:27)

F. What does Romans contribute to God's big picture?

1. God's Righteousness _____ in his universal plan (1:18–8:39)

the _____ for God's Righteousness (1:18-3:20), the _____ of

God's Righteousness (3:21–4:25), and the _____ of God's

Righteousness (5:1–8:39)

Romans 3:21–24 (NET Bible)	**Romans 8:1–4** (NET Bible)
But now apart from the law the righteousness of God (which is attested by the law and the prophets) has been disclosed– namely, the righteousness of God through the faithfulness of Jesus *who is the* Christ for all who believe. For there is no distinction, for all have sinned and fall short of the glory of God. But they are justified freely by his grace through the redemption that is in Christ Jesus.	There is therefore now no condemnation for those who are in Christ Jesus. For the law of the life-giving Spirit in Christ Jesus has set you free from the law of sin and death. For God achieved what the law could not do because it was weakened through the flesh. By sending his own Son in the likeness of sinful flesh and concerning sin, he condemned sin in the flesh, so that the righteous requirement of the law may be fulfilled in us, who do not walk according to the flesh but according to the Spirit.

2. Precepts for righteousness in _____ _____ (12:1–15:13) before

God (12:1-2), in the _____ (12:3–21), in _____ (13:1–14),

and when differences occur among believers (14:1–15:13)

Life-Style within the Church	**Life-Style within Society**
Love must be without hypocrisy. Be devoted to one another with mutual love, showing eagerness in honoring one another. Bless those who persecute you, bless and do not curse. Live in harmony with one another; do not be haughty but associate with the lowly. If possible, so far as it depends on you, live peaceably with all people. Do not avenge yourselves, dear friends, but give place to God's wrath, for it is written, "*Vengeance is mine, I will repay*," says the Lord. Do not be overcome by evil, but overcome evil with good.	Let every person be subject to the governing authorities (even when a liberal is in office). For there is no authority except by God's appointment . . . So the person who resists such authority resists the ordinance of God, and those who resist will incur judgment (for rulers cause no fear for good conduct but for bad). For this reason you also pay taxes, for the authorities are God's servants devoted to governing. Pay everyone what is owed: taxes to whom taxes are due, revenue to whom revenue is due, respect to whom respect is due, honor to whom honor is due. Owe no one anything, except to love one another, for the one who loves his neighbor has fulfilled the law. For the commandments, "***Do not commit adultery, do not murder, do not steal, do not covet***," (and if there is any other commandment) are summed up in this, "***Love your neighbor as yourself***." Love does no wrong to a neighbor. Therefore love is the fulfillment of the law.

CONCLUSION

Matthew's contribution to God's big picture is simply this: knowing about our Messiah's life, example, and kingdom teachings affirms his disciples, empowers his disciples to live as kingdom saints, emboldens his disciples to proclaim the kingdom message, and energizes his disciples to stand firm for the kingdom despite any conflict or rejection.

Paul's letter to the Romans contributes to God's big picture in this way: God's righteousness was exercised on behalf all people so that all those who claim to follow Jesus, the Messiah, might execute a life of righteousness.

SERIES EDITOR

Benjamin L. Merkle (PhD, Southern Baptist Theological Seminary) is professor of New Testament Greek at Southeastern Baptist Theological Seminary and is the author of *40 Questions About Elders and Deacons.*

AVAILABLE

40 Questions About Christians and Biblical Law
Thomas R. Schreiner
978-0-8254-3891-2 • Paperback • 256 pages • $17.99

40 Questions About Creation and Evolution
Kenneth Keathley, Mark F. Rooker
978-0-8254-2941-5 • Paperback • 432 pages • $19.99

40 Questions About Elders and Deacons
Benjamin L. Merkle
978-0-8254-3364-1 • Paperback • 272 pages • $17.99

40 Questions About Interpreting the Bible
Robert L. Plummer
978-0-8254-3498-3 • Paperback • 352 pages • $17.99

40 Questions About the End Times
Eckhard J. Schnabel
978-0-8254-3896-7 • Paperback • 352 pages • $17.99

40 Questions About the Historical Jesus
C. Marvin Pate
978-0-8254-4284-1 • Paperback • 416 pages • $19.99

FORTHCOMING

40 Questions About Baptism and the Lord's Supper
John S. Hammett

40 Questions About Election and Atonement
Bruce A. Ware

40 Questions About Heaven and Hell
Alan W. Gomes

40 Questions About Marriage, Divorce, and Remarriage
Jim Newheiser

40 Questions About Salvation
Matthew Barrett and Gregg R. Allison

40 Questions About the Text and Canon of the New Testament
Daniel B. Wallace

Kregel Academic • Rights: World

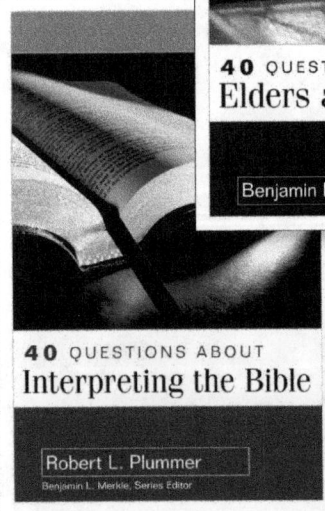

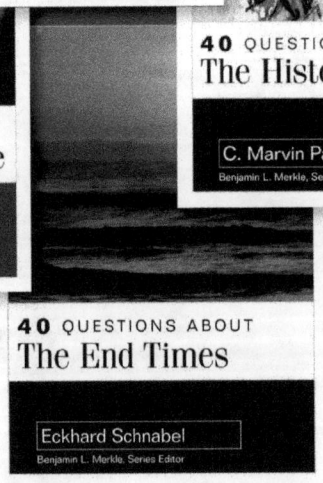

40 Questions Series
Benjamin L. Merkle, series editor

The 40 Questions series presents excellent research in accessible language and clear writing. Designed for both students and thoughtful general readers, these resources help readers make sense of the Bible's most difficult topics.

GOD'S FUTURE STORY

by Aaron C. Peer

I. INTRODUCTION

When we talk about God's future story, what books of the Bible or parts of the Bible address that topic?

A. Daniel 2, 7-12

B. Various passages from the major and minor prophets

C. Jesus' Olivet Discourse (Matt. 24:1-25:46; Mark 13; Luke 21:5-36)

D. 1 Thessalonians 4-5

E. 2 Thessalonians 2

F. Various other New Testament passages

And of course . . .

The book of Revelation tells us a great deal about God's future story, but it reads less like a

_____ and more like a _____.

II. WHAT IS THE SUBJECT OF REVELATION?

A. The book of Revelation is a _____ between two opposing citizenships:

Two Cities	_____	or	_____
Two Women	_____	or	_____
Two Kingdoms	_____	or	_____

B. The question that John wants his readers to answer is . . .

To which group do you belong? And if you say that you belong to the kingdom of God, then are you living out the values of the world or kingdom values?

Greeting	"To the angel in the church of Ephesus write. . ."
Jesus' Self-Description	"These are the words of him who holds the seven stars in his right hand and walks among the seven golden lampstands."
Commendation	"I know your deeds, your hard work and your perseverance. I know that you cannot tolerate wicked people, that you have tested those who claim to be apostles but are not, and have found them false. You have persevered and have endured hardships for my name, and have not grown weary."
Condemnation	"Yet I hold this against you: You have forsaken the love you had at first."
Warning	"Consider how far you have fallen! Repent and do the things you did at first. If you do not repent, I will come to you and remove your lampstand from its place. But you have this in your favor: You hate the practices of the Nicolaitans, which I also hate."
Exhortation	"Whoever has ears, let them hear what the Spirit says to the churches."
Promise to the Overcomer	"To the one who is victorious, I will give the right to eat from the tree of life, which is in the paradise of God." (NET Bilbe)

For Further Reading: Here is the general pattern of each letter in Revelation 2-3. *This example is taken from Revelation 2:1–7. Notice that the thrust of the letters is to encourage the Asian believers to overcome the world's values and to stick with Jesus.*

1. What will happen to . . .

    . . . The Citizens of Babylon: They will fail and be _____ .

    . . . The Citizens of Jerusalem: They will be _____ and live in paradise with God forever.

2. Why does John lay out a vision of the future then?

John wants them to overcome the _____ in their hearts and

lives and remain faithful to the Kingdom of God and live out its values.

Here is an example of John encouraging his readers to leave Babylon behind:

Revelation 18:2-5 (NET Bible)

"Fallen, fallen, is Babylon the great!
She has become a lair for demons,
a haunt for every unclean spirit,
a haunt for every unclean bird,
a haunt for every unclean and detested beast.

For all the nations have fallen from the wine of her immoral
passion, and the kings of the earth have committed sexual
immorality with her, and the merchants of the earth have gotten
rich from the power of her sensual behavior."

Then I heard another voice from heaven saying, "***Come out of
her***, my people, so you will not ta part in her sins and so you will
not receive her plagues, because her sins have piled up all the way
to heaven and God has remembered her crimes.

The Subject of Revelation Summarized: John wants his readers to _____

Babylon (the world) and to remain faithful to Jesus.

III. WHAT IS THE OCCASION? WHY DOES JOHN WRITE REVELATION?

John is worried that external and internal _____ are leading the

believers in Asia Minor away from Jesus and his kingdom.

A. Pressure from _____ :

Revelation 2:8-10 (NET Bible)

"To the angel of the church in Smyrna write the following:

"This is the solemn pronouncement of the one who is the first and the last, the one who was dead, but came to life: 'I know the distress you are suffering and your poverty (but you are rich). I also know the slander against you by those who call themselves Jews and really are not, but are a synagogue of Satan. Do not be afraid of the things you are about to suffer. The devil is about to have some of you thrown into prison so you may be tested, and you will experience suffering for ten days. Remain *faithful* even to the point of death, and I will give you the crown that is life itself.

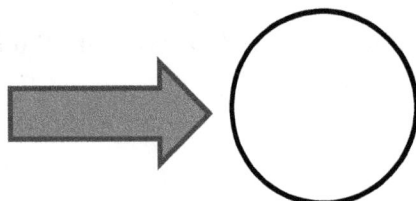

B. Pressure from _____:

Revelation 2:20-26 (NET Bible)

But I have this against you: You tolerate that woman Jezebel, who calls herself a prophetess, and by her teaching deceives my servants to commit sexual immorality and to eat food sacrificed to idols. I have given her time to repent, but she is not willing to repent of her sexual immorality. Look! I am throwing her onto a bed of violent illness, and those who commit adultery with her into terrible suffering, unless they repent of her deeds. Furthermore, I will strike her followers with a deadly disease, and then all the churches will know that I am the one who searches minds and hearts. I will repay each one of you what your deeds deserve. But to the rest of you in Thyatira, all who do not hold to this teaching (who have not learned the so-called "deep secrets of Satan"), to you I say: I do not put any additional burden on you. However, hold on to what you have until I come. And to the one who conquers and who continues in my deeds until the end, I will give him authority over the nations

The occasion for John Summarized: John is moved to write because he is worried about persecution from the _____ and temptation from the _____ moving the believers away from Jesus and his kingdom.

For Further Reading: Take a look at John's recurrent encouragements to overcome the pressures and temptations of the world: Revelation 2:7, 11, 17, 25-28; 3:5, 12, 20-21; 13:6-10; 14:12; 16:15; 18:4; 22:11, 12. cf. 1 John 2:14-17.

IV. WHAT IS JOHN'S INTENTION IN WRITING?

A. The _____ Purpose of Revelation

Revelation 1:1-3 (NET Bible)

The revelation of Jesus Christ, which God gave him to show his servants what must happen very soon. He made it clear by sending his angel to his servant John, who then testified to everything that he saw concerning the word of God and the testimony about Jesus Christ. Blessed is the one who reads the words of this prophecy aloud, and blessed are those who hear and obey the things written in it, because the time is near!

John's stated purpose is that he wants his readers to understand the _____.

B. The _____ Purposes of Revelation

BUT . . . why does he want them to understand the future?

1. John wants both the citizens of the Kingdom of God and the citizens of the _____ to know where their citizenship will take them in the future!

2. John wants to encourage the believers in light of this future to remain _____ to Jesus no matter the consequences.

C. The _____ of the purpose of Revelation (The how)

1. John reminds them that _____ is the one in charge, the king.

2. John explains to them that he is moving history toward its _____.

3. John points out that the faithful will be _____ and the wicked will be _____.

John's Intention Summarized: John intends to remind his readers that their true citizenship has eternal _____, by reminding them that God is in charge, that he is moving history toward its culmination, and that the _____ will be rewarded and the unfaithful will be punished.

V.   WHAT ARE SOME KEY VERSES TO UNDERSTANDING REVELATION?

Revelation 1:7
(NET Bible)

Look! *He is returning with the clouds,* and *every eye will see him, even those who pierced him,* and all the tribes on the earth will mourn because of him. This will certainly come to pass! Amen.

Revelation 3:11-12, 21
(NET Bible)

I am coming soon. *Hold on to what you have,* so that no one will take your crown. *The one who is victorious* I will make a pillar in the temple of my God. Never again will they leave it. I will write on them the name of my God and the name of the city of my God, the new Jerusalem, which is coming down out of heaven from my God; and I will also write on them my new name.

To the *one who is victorious*, I will give the right to sit with me on my throne, just as I was victorious and sat down with my Father on his throne.

Revelation 21:6-8
(NET Bible)

He said to me: "It is done. I am the Alpha and the Omega, the Beginning and the End. To the thirsty I will give water without cost from the spring of the water of life. *Those who are victorious* will inherit all this, *and I will be their God and they will be my children.* But the cowardly, the unbelieving, the vile, the murderers, the sexually immoral, those who practice magic arts, the idolaters and all liars—they will be consigned to the fiery lake of burning sulfur. This is the second death."

Understanding Revelation Summarized: The key to unlocking Revelation is to understand that John is giving us a glorious _____ of the future to encourage us to hold on to Jesus in the present even when we face pressure and temptation.

VI.   WHAT IS THE LITERARY FLOW OF REVELATION?

   A. Prologue (1:1-3)

   B. Vision of the Son of Man among the seven churches (1:4-3:22)

   C. Vision of the Lamb and the seven sealed scroll, trumpets, and bowls (4:1-16:21)

      1. The vision of God's throne (4)

      2. The vision of the Lamb (5)

      3. The seal judgments (6)

         Interlude #1 - The sealed and the multitude (7:1-17)

      4. The trumpet judgments (8-9, 11:15-19)

         Interlude #2 - The giant angel and the two witnesses (10:1-11:14)

         Interlude #3 - The beast from the earth, the beast from the sea, and

            winepress of God's fury (12:1-14:20)

      5. The bowl judgments (15-16)

    D. Vision of the Christ's return (17:1-19:21)

    E. Vision of the new heaven and the new earth (20:1-22:5)

    F. Epilogue: Christ's reassurance that he is coming quickly (22:6-21)

For Further Outlines: See Mark Wilson's *Charts on the Book of Revelation: Literary, Historical, and Theological Perspectives* in Kregel Charts of the Bible and Theology (Grand Rapids: Kregel, 2007).

VII. WHAT ARE SOME OF JOHN'S MAIN THEMES?

A. The _____ of the Lamb

JESUS IS THE MAIN CHARACTER!

Jesus is . . .

... the transcendent one (Revelation 1)

... the one who patiently walks among the churches (Revelation 2-3)

... the lion of Judah (Revelation 5)

... the root of Jesse (Revelation 5)

... the lamb (Revelation 5) *see example*

... the shepherd (Revelation 7) *see example*

... the king who reigns forever (Revelation 11)

... the son who thwarts the dragon (Revelation 12)

Revelation 5:9-10 – *The Lamb*

They were singing a new song:

"You are worthy to take the scroll and to open its seals because you were killed, and at the cost of your own blood you have purchased for God persons from every tribe, language, people, and nation. You have appointed them as a kingdom and priests to serve our God, and they will reign on the earth." (NET Bible)

Revelation 7:15-17 – *The Shepherd*

For this reason they are before the throne of God, and they serve him day and night in his temple, and the one seated on the throne will shelter them. *They will never go hungry or be thirsty again and the sun will not beat down on them, nor any burning heat*, because the Lamb in the middle of the throne will shepherd them and lead them to springs of living water, *and God will wipe away every tear from their eyes*." (NET Bible)

Jesus is . . .

. . . the reason the saints are able to thwart the dragon (Revelation 12) *see example*

. . . the faithful and true one (Revelation 19)

. . . the word of God (Revelation 19)

. . . the one who sets the scales straight (Revelation 19)

. . . the lamp (Revelation 21)

Revelation 12:10-11 – *The reason saints can beat down Satan*

Then I heard a loud voice in heaven saying,

"The salvation and the power and the kingdom of our God, and the ruling authority of his Christ, have now come, because the accuser of our brothers and sisters, the one who accuses them day and night before our God, has been thrown down. But they overcame him by the blood of the Lamb and by the word of their testimony, and they did not love their lives so much that they were afraid to die. (NET Bible)

All of this is a fulfillment of which covenant? _____

For Further Reading: Take a look at all of the fulfillment language for the Davidic Covenant that we find in Revelation: 1:5-6; 2:13, 26-27; 3:7, 14, 21; 5:5, 10; 11:15-18; 12:5, 10-12; 14:14; 17:14; 19:6, 11-19; 20:4; 22:4, 16. For a reminder of the promises and language of the Davidic covenant see 2 Samuel 7.

B. The faithful must _____

Revelation 14:12 (NET Bible)	This requires the steadfast endurance of the saints – those who obey God's commandments and hold to their faith in Jesus.
Revelation 15:2-3 (NET Bible)	Then I saw something like a sea of glass mixed with fire, and those who had conquered the beast and his image and the number of his name. They were standing by the sea of glass, holding harps given to them by God. They sang the song of Moses the servant of God and the song of the Lamb:

"Great and astounding are your deeds, Lord God, the All-Powerful!
Just and true are your ways, King over the nations! |
| **Revelation 20:4-6** (NET Bible) | Then I saw thrones and seated on them were those who had been given authority to judge. I also saw the souls of those who had been beheaded because of the testimony about Jesus and because of the word of God. These had not worshiped the beast or his image and had refused to receive his mark on their forehead or hand. They came to life and reigned with Christ for a thousand years. (The rest of the dead did not come to life until the thousand years were |

finished.) This is the first resurrection. Blessed and holy is the one who takes part in the first resurrection. The second death has no power over them, but they will be priests of God and of Christ, and they will reign with him for a thousand years.

All of this is a fulfillment of which covenant? _____

For Further Reading: Take a look at all of the fulfillment language for the Abrahamic Covenant that we find in Revelation: 4:10; 5:9; 7:9; 10:11; 14:6; 15:4; 21:14. For a reminder of the promises and language of the Abrahamic covenant see Genesis 12:1-3 and 15:18-21.

C. All things will soon be _____

What is THE covenant promise, which takes on a new dimension every time we are introduced to a newer covenant?

Leviticus _____: "I will put my dwelling place among you, and I will be your God, and you will be my people"

When Jesus comes again, this promise will be completely and finally fulfilled:

Revelation 21:1-4 (NET Bible)	Then I saw a new heaven and a new earth, for the first heaven and earth had ceased to exist, and the sea existed no more. And I saw the holy city – the new Jerusalem – descending out of heaven from God, made ready like a bride adorned for her husband. And I heard a loud voice from the throne saying: "Look! The residence of God is among human beings. He will live among them, and they will be his people, and God himself will be with them. He will wipe away every tear from their eyes, and death will not exist anymore – or mourning, or crying, or pain, for the former things have ceased to exist."
Revelation 21:22-27 (NET Bible)	Now I saw no temple in the city, because the Lord God – the All-Powerful – and the Lamb are its temple. The city does not need the sun or the moon to shine on it, because the glory of God lights it up, and its lamp is the Lamb. The nations will walk by its light and the kings of the earth will bring their grandeur into it. Its gates will never be closed during the day (and there will be no night there). They will bring the grandeur and the wealth of the nations into it, but nothing ritually unclean will not ever enter into it or anyone who does what is detestable or practices falsehood, but only those whose names are written in the Lamb's book of life.
Revelation 22:1-5 (NET Bible)	Then the angel showed me the river of the water of life – water as clear as crystal – pouring out from the throne of God and of the Lamb, flowing down

the middle of the city's main street. On each side of the river is the tree of life producing twelve kinds of fruit, yielding its fruit every month of the year. Its leaves are for the healing of the nations. And there will no longer be any curse, and the throne of God and the Lamb will be in the city. His servants will worship him, and they will see his face, and his name will be on their foreheads. Night will be no more, and they will not need the light of a lamp or the light of the sun, because the Lord God will shine on them, and they will reign forever and ever.

All of this is a fulfillment of which covenant? _____

For Further Reading: Take a look at all of the fulfillment language for the New Covenant that we find in Revelation: 1:5, 5:9; 7:15-17; 12:11; 14:3-4; 21:22-27. For a reminder of the promises and language of the New covenant see Jeremiah 31:31-34.

For Further Reading: Take a look at the imagery on how the consummation of God's story will return us back to Eden-like conditions see Revelation 1:18; 2:7-8; 3:12; 4:10; 14:13; 20:14; 22:1-4.

Sources Consulted

Aune, David E. Revelation 1–5 in Word Biblical Commentary. Edited by Ralph P. Martin and Lynn Allan Losie. Dallas, TX: Word Biblical commentary ,1997.

Bateman IV, Herbert W. *Interpreting the General Letters: An Exegetical Handbook.* Volume 3. Handbooks for New Testament Exegesis, Edited by John D. Harvey. Grand Rapids: Kregel, 2013.

Bateman IV, Herbert W. Darrell L. Bock, Gordon H. Johnston. *Jesus the Messiah: Tracing the Promises, Expectations, and Coming of Israel's King.* Grand Rapids: Kregel, 2012.

Bateman IV, Herbert W. and D. Brent Sandy, editors. *Interpreting the Psalms for Preaching and Teaching.* St. Louis, MO: Chaalice Press, 2010.

Beale, G. K. *The Book of Revelation.* The New International Greek Testament Commentary. Edited by I. Howard Marshall and Donald A. Hagner. Grand Rapids: Zondervan, 1999.

Bultmann, Rudolf. *The History of the Synoptic Tradition.* Revised Edition. New York, NY: Harper and Row, 1963.

Carson, D. A. and Douglas J. Moo. *An Introduction to the New Testament.* Second Edition. Grand Rapids: Zondervan, 1992, 2005.

Chisholm, Robert B. *Interpreting the Historical Books: An Exegetical Handbook.* Volume 2. Handbooks for Old Testament Exegesis. Edited by David M. Howard Jr. Grand Rapids: Kregel, 2009.

Currid, John D. *Against the Gods.* Wheaton, IL: Crossway, 2013.

Davis, John J. *Birth of a Kingdom.* Winona Lake, IN: BMH Books, 1998.

_____. *From Paradise to Prison.* Winona Lake, IN: BMH Books, 1998.

Elwell, Walter A. and Robert W. Yarbrough. *Encountering the New Testament: A Historical and Theological Survey.* Grand Rapids: Baker, 1998.

Guthrie, Donald. *New Testament Introduction.* Revised Edition. Downers Grove, IL: InterVarsity Press, fourth ed.1990.

Harvey, John D. *Interpreting the Pauline Letters: An Exegetical Handbook.* Volume 2. Handbooks for New Testament Exegesis. Grand Rapids: Kregel, 2012.

Lewis, C. S. *The Weight of Glory.* San Francisco, CA: Harper San Francisco, 2001.

Merrill, Eugene H. *Kingdom of Priests: A History of Old Testament Israel.* Grand Rapids: Baker, 1987.

Mounce, Robert H. *The Book of Revelation.* The New International Commentary on the New Testament. Edited by Ned B. Stonehouse, F. F. Bruce, Gordon D. Fee. Grand Rapids: Eerdmans, 1977.

Schreiner, Thomas R. *Romans*. Baker Exegetical Commentary on the New Testament. Grand Rapids, Baker, 1998.

Stott, John. *Romans: God's Good News for the World*. Downeres Grove, IL: InterVarsity Academic, 1994.

Turner, David L. *Matthew*. Baker Exegetical Commentary on the New Testament. Grand Rapids, Baker, 2008.

Vanhoozer, Kevin J., ed. *Theological Interpretation of the Old Testament*. Grand Rapids: Baker, 2008.

Vogt, Peter T. *Interpreting the Pentateuch: An Exegetical Handbook*. Volume 1. Handbooks for Old Testament Exegesis. Edited by David M. Howard Jr. Grand Rapids: Kregel, 2009.

Waltke, Bruce K. *An Old Testament Theology*. Grand Rapids: Zondervan, 2011.

Walton, John H. *Ancient Near Eastern Thought and the Old Testament*. Grand Rapids: Baker, 2006.

Walvoord, John F. and Roy B. Zuck. *The Bible Knowledge Commentary: Old Testament*. Wheaton, IL: Victor Books, 1985.

Wenham, Gordon. *The Psalter Reclaimed*. Wheaton, IL: Crossway, 2013.

Wilson, Mark. *Charts on the Book of Revelation*. Kregel Charts of the Bible and Theology. Grand Rapids: Kregel, 2007.

Wright, Christopher J. H. *The Mission of God*. Downers Grove, IL: InterVarsity Academic, 2006.

EXEGETICAL GUIDES FOR TRANSLATING THE NEW TESTAMENT

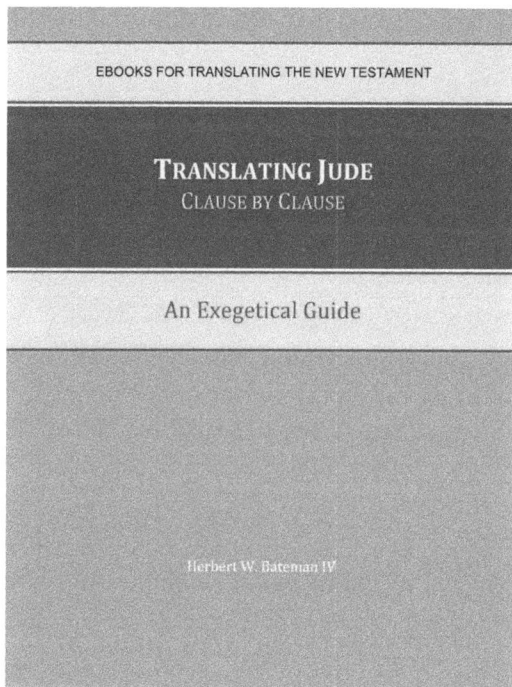

EBOOKS FOR TRANSLATING THE NEW TESTAMENT

TRANSLATING JUDE
CLAUSE BY CLAUSE

An Exegetical Guide

Herbert W. Bateman IV

Designed as a translational guide, these CYBER-CENTER FOR BIBLICAL STUDIES eBooks for translating the New Testament isolates usage of independent and dependent clauses, provides tips for translating New Testament letters, and shares exegetical explanations to assist in the translation of biblical letters. Each book divides into three parts. First, an introduction prepares the reader for translating the letters. Second, letters are divided into manageable units of thought for translation purposes while providing contextual orientation for each unit. Finally, an answer keys are provided with detailed exegetical explanations about each author's divisions and translations of the text.

Each book interacts with lexicons, grammars, and English translations in order to orient the reader / translator to the challenges that come with translating New Testament letters. Yet the contextual orientation and clausal outlines enable the reader/translator to trace the author's flow of thought in a manner that will be helpful for teaching and preaching purposes.

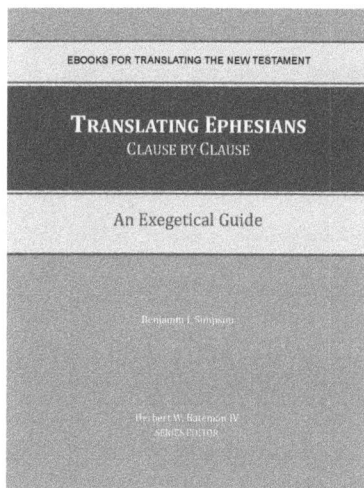

EBOOKS FOR TRANSLATING THE NEW TESTAMENT

TRANSLATING EPHESIANS
CLAUSE BY CLAUSE

An Exegetical Guide

Benjamin I. Simpson

Herbert W. Bateman IV
SERIES EDITOR

by Benjamin I. Simpson

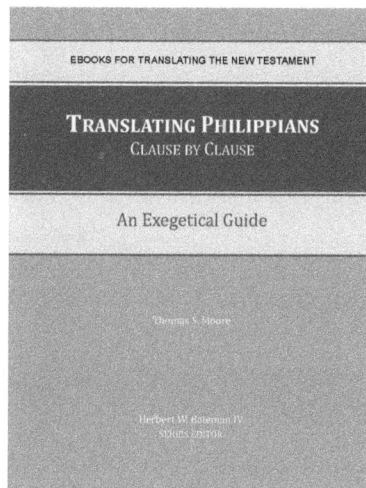

EBOOKS FOR TRANSLATING THE NEW TESTAMENT

TRANSLATING PHILIPPIANS
CLAUSE BY CLAUSE

An Exegetical Guide

Thomas S. Moore

Herbert W. Bateman IV
SERIES EDITOR

by Thomas S. Moore

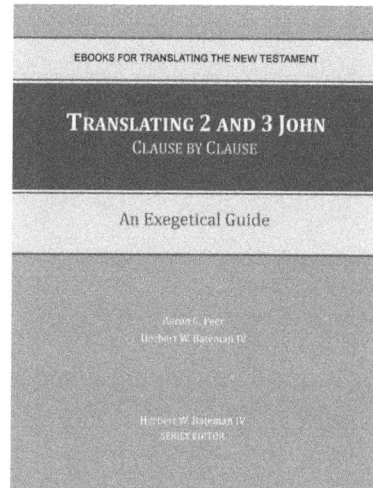

EBOOKS FOR TRANSLATING THE NEW TESTAMENT

TRANSLATING 2 AND 3 JOHN
CLAUSE BY CLAUSE

An Exegetical Guide

Aaron C. Peer
Herbert W. Bateman IV

Herbert W. Bateman IV
SERIES EDITOR

by Aaron C. Peer
Herbert W. Bateman IV

All eBooks for Translating the New Testament are available on Amazon.

www.ingramcontent.com/pod-product-compliance
Lightning Source LLC
Chambersburg PA
CBHW080937040426
42443CB00015B/3456